EXPLORING

SOUTHERN VECTIS

COUNTRY

• A PAST AND PRESENT COMPANION •

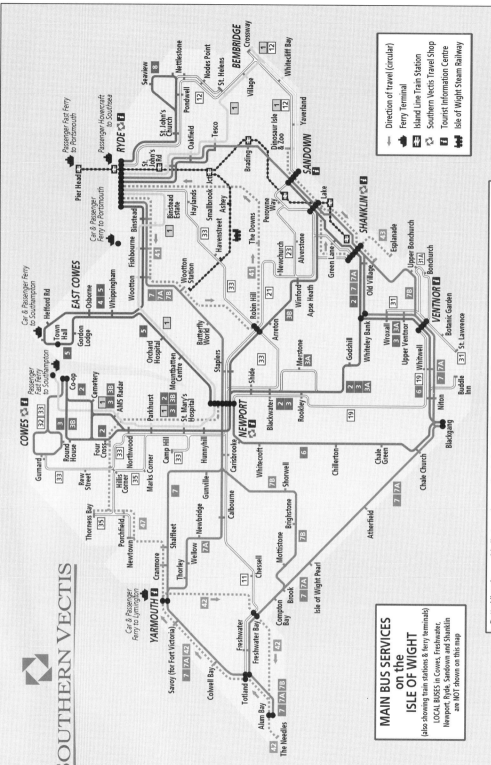

SOUTHERN VECTIS

MAIN BUS SERVICES on the ISLE OF WIGHT

(also showing train stations & ferry terminals)

LOCAL BUSES in Cowes, Freshwater, Newport, Ryde, Sandown and Shanklin are NOT shown on this map

Routes correct at April 2003

Dotted lines (■ ■ ■ ■) indicate services running during SUMMER only : Hollow lines (══════) indicate an infrequent or limited service

The following services do NOT run at all on SUNDAYS : 11 19 21 23 31 31A 32 35

Direction of travel (circular)

Ferry Terminal

Island Line Train Station

Southern Vectis Travel Shop

Tourist Information Centre

Isle of Wight Steam Railway

Cartography © Southern Vectis 2003

EXPLORING

SOUTHERN VECTIS

COUNTRY

• A PAST AND PRESENT COMPANION •

Chris Harris

• TOWN AND COUNTRY HERITAGE •
from
The NOSTALGIA *Collection*

First published in 2003

British Library Cataloguing in Publication Data

A catalogue record for this book is available from the British Library.

ISBN 1 85895 188 7

Past & Present Publishing Ltd
The Trundle
Ringstead Road
Great Addington
Kettering
Northants NN14 4BW

Tel/Fax: 01536 330588
email: sales@nostalgiacollection.com
Website: www.nostalgiacollection.com

Printed and bound in Great Britain

Acknowledgements

It would have been impossible to produce this book without the help that has been readily and cheerfully given by many people. Marc Morgan Huws, Commercial and Operations Manager of Southern Vectis, agreed that I could use the Company's corporate identity for the book and very kindly lent me a number of historic photographs. Thanks also to Ed Wills, Operations Co-ordinator of Southern Vectis, for supplying the map. Philip Davies from Ferndown was kind enough to give me access to his entire (and very extensive) collection of Southern Vectis photographs. Brian Jackson from Weymouth supplied photographs of the last days of the Isle of Wight steam locomotives, and thanks also to R. K. Blencowe and to Photobus for permission to reproduce material.

For many of the general views and street scenes, I give particular thanks to Richard Smout, the Isle of Wight Council Archivist, for allowing me to use a number of the photographs held at the Record Office at Newport; the identity of some of the photographers was not known, but notice was given in the *Isle of Wight County Press* and the *London Gazette* of the intention to use the images in this way. Dave and Betty Underwood of Classic Pictures in Christchurch kindly loaned a further selection of interesting views.

Many people have supplied helpful information, including Gill Lee from Brading, Jack Toogood from Sandown and Peter Trevaskis from Normandy, Guildford. To these, and to others who have helped, my very grateful thanks.

Contents

9   **Newport, Merstone, Godshill, Whitwell, Niton, Ventnor**   **9**

DAILY.

		NSu	NSu	NSu	NSu			NSu		NSu		NSu	
		am	am	am	am	am	pm	pm	pm	pm	pm	pm	pm
Newport (St. James's Square) ... dep		6 45	7 50	9 30	1130	......	1 30	4 30	5 30	6 5	......	......	
Blackwater (Corner)	,,	6 52	7 57	9 37	1137	......	1 37	4 37	5 37	6 12	......	......	
Merstone (Station)	,,	7 0	8 5	9 45	1145	......	1 45	4 45	5 45	6 14	......	......	
Godshill (Scotland Corner)	,,	7 6	8 11	9 51	1151	......	1 51	4 51	5 51	......	......	......	
Whitwell (Church)	,,	7 16	8 21	10 1	12 1	......	2 1	5 1	6 1	......	......	......	
Niton (Bus Shelter)	,,	7 21	8 26	10 6	12 6	1 6	2 6	5 6	6 6	......	9 6	1011	
Whitwell (Church)	,,	7 26	8 31	1011	1211	1 11	2 11	5 11	6 11	......	9 11	1016	
Ventnor (Pine Point)	,,	7 34	8 39	1019	1219	1 19	2 19	5 19	6 19	......	9 19	1024	
Ventnor (Town Hall) ... arr		7 40	8*45	1025	1225	1 25	2 25	5 25	6 25	......	9 25	1030	

		NSu	NSu	NSu	NSu	NSu	NSu			NSu				S
		am	am	am	am	am	am	pm	pm	pm	pm	pm	pm	pm
Ventnor (Town Hall) dep		6 21	......	7 45	9 0	1030	1230	1 30	4*30	5 30	6 35	9 30	10 30	
Ventnor (Pine Point)	,,	6 27	......	7 51	9 6	1036	1236	1 36	4 36	5 36	6 41	9 36	10 36	
Whitwell (Church)	,,	6 35	......	7 59	9 14	1044	1244	1 44	4 44	5 44	6 49	9 44	10 44	
Niton (Bus Shelter)	,,	6 40	......	8 4	9 19	1049	1249	1 49	4 49	5 49	7†	2 9	49	......
Whitwell (Church)	,,	......	......	8 9	9 24	1054	......	1 54	4 54	5 54	7 7	......	10 44	
Godshill (Scotland Corner)	,,	......	......	8 19	9 34	11 4	......	2 4	5 4	6 4	7 17	......	10‡54	
Merstone (Station)	,,	......	7 3	8 25	9 40	1110	......	2 10	5 10	6 10	7 23	......	......	
Blackwater (Corner)	,,	......	7 11	8 33	9 48	1118	......	2 18	5 18	6 18	7 31	......	......	
Newport (St. James's Square) ... arr		......	7 18	8 40	9 55	1125	......	2 25	5 25	6 25	7 38	......	......	

NSu—Not Sundays.   S—Saturdays.   †—Arrives 6.54 p.m.

*—Runs to/from Ventnor Secondary Modern School on Schooldays.   ‡—Continues to Shanklin on Service 6

September 1956

Before we commence our exploration of the Isle of Wight, let us compare the Southern Vectis buses we could use for our travels, past and present. Very representative of the first 20 or so years after the Second World War is fleet number 727 (FDL 295). This Bristol K5G with 55-seat lowbridge bodywork by Eastern Coach Works was new in September 1948 and was in service with Southern Vectis until 1964. It is seen here at Shanklin Bus Station (now demolished – see page 50) operating Service 22 to Sandown.

The first low-floor easy-access buses joined the Southern Vectis fleet in 2002, when on Friday 18 October seven double-deck Volvo B7TL buses with Plaxton 73-seat bodywork, together with one Dennis Dart Saloon with 29-seat bodywork also by Plaxton, were officially launched by Councillor Ernie Fox, the Isle of Wight Council's Executive Member for Transport. Two days later one of the new double-deck buses, fleet number 101 (HW52 EPL) was photographed next to the new saloon, fleet number 300 (HW52 EPX), on display to the public at Newport Quay. These eight new buses represent an investment of more than £1 million. *Philip Davies Collection/CH*

Introduction

Having enjoyed compiling *Exploring Wilts & Dorset Country* in 1999 and *Exploring Solent Blue Line Country* in 2001, I have now taken the logical step of crossing the Solent to the Isle of Wight to explore the area served by Solent Blue Line's parent company, Southern Vectis.

The origins of Southern Vectis go back to October 1921 when Dodson & Campbell Limited commenced operations between Cowes and Newport. In 1922 the Company became Dodson Brothers Limited, trading as Vectis Bus Service. The buses carried a blue, red and white livery and carried the fleet name in gold ('Vectis' is the Roman name for the Isle of Wight). Half of the share capital of the Company was acquired by the Southern Railway in 1929, and the fleet name was changed to Southern Vectis in 1930, but the original livery was retained until 1932, buses thereafter being painted green and cream. With the nationalisation of the railways in 1948, Southern Vectis also became state-owned, in due course becoming part of the National Bus Company in 1969. The 1985 Transport Act provided for the break-up and sale of the National Bus Company, and Southern Vectis returned to private ownership on 7 October 1986 following a management buy-out.

In this book we take a nostalgic tour around some of the places served by Southern Vectis. Photographs taken between 1889 and 1985 are paired with photographs of the same locations taken during 2002, or in a few cases January 2003. Whether you remember the Island as it was in days gone by, or whether you are curious about the appearance of places in the past, this book should be of interest. The final chapter takes a look at all forms of public transport on the Island, including the links with the mainland. In this regard I should say that where I have commented on various types of buses the opinions given are personal, but based on 30 years' experience in the bus industry with Hants & Dorset Motor Services and the Wilts & Dorset Bus Company.

I have thoroughly enjoyed researching and putting together *Exploring Southern Vectis Country* – I hope you will derive similar enjoyment from reading the book.

Chris Harris
Poole, Dorset

June 1955

Many visitors to the Isle of Wight arrive as foot passengers on the crossing from Portsmouth to Ryde. In 1954 Southern Vectis opened a summer season tours booking kiosk at Ryde Pier Head – an excellent location to attract custom from visitors as they arrived from the boats. This photograph dates from 1960 and shows the splendid contemporary design of the kiosk. The prices are interesting too – a day tour round the Island by luxury coach cost 11 shillings (55p), while an afternoon tour to Alum Bay and The Needles was a mere 7 shillings (35p)!

'See the Island by Southern Vectis' exhorts the fascia – let us now do just that as we explore Southern Vectis Country, past and present. *Southern Vectis Collection.*

Newport

NEWPORT BUS STATION could be described as the hub of the Southern Vectis bus network. For many years the main bus terminus in Newport was at St James Square, but the present bus station in South Street was opened on 18 May 1962 by the then Mayor of Newport, Alderman E. W. G. Hands JP. The 'past' photograph shows the bus station when newly opened. Visible in the left foreground is the front of a Bristol Lodekka, while fleet number 740 (GDL 713) is ready to operate a journey on Service 13 to Gurnard. This Bristol KS5G was new in November 1950 and remained in service with Southern Vectis until February 1967. In the background we see part of a Bedford OB that has been downgraded from coach to bus duties, and painted in the green bus livery. On the right a lady wearing a headscarf is subjecting the timetables for Services 3, 5 and 6 to very close scrutiny!

The location is readily recognised in the 'present' photograph, taken on Saturday 18 January 2003, although additional shelters and railings have been provided along the island platform on the right, obscuring the view of part of the building. In the left foreground we see a low-floor Volvo B7TL double-deck bus, new in October 2002 (see also page 6), loading passengers for the 12.20pm departure on Service 7 for Yarmouth. The 33-seat Dennis Dart, N814 PDL, new in May 1996, will operate the 12.18pm departure on Service 1 to Ryde and Bembridge.
Southern Vectis Collection/CH

HIGH STREET: These photographs were taken looking east along Newport High Street from close to its junction with St James Street. In the left foreground of the 'past' photograph, which dates from the late 1940s, is the Bugle Hotel. Once an important coaching inn and staging post, this historic hotel was closed in 1989, and it can be seen in the 'present' photograph, taken on Saturday 6 July 2002, that the ground floor units are now occupied by a Mothercare shop and by Ottakars bookshop. On the other side of the street, what was A. G. Bird's stationery shop is now a Thomas Cook travel agency, while the premises formerly occupied by a decorators' merchants has been rebuilt and is now an Adams clothing store.

The parking signs incorporated a hinged flap so that they could show either 'No Waiting' or 'Waiting Limited' (to a given period of time, eg 30 minutes). The practice of allowing parking on each side of the street on alternate days was once very common. In 2002 parking is permitted on both sides of the street, but as can be seen from the signs motorists now have to pay for the privilege! *Isle of Wight Record Office/CH*

HIGH STREET: These photographs also look east along Newport High Street, but are taken from a point closer to the Guildhall than the views opposite. In this case the 'past' photograph was taken around 1970, and in general the scene is readily recognised in the 'present' view, taken on Saturday 6 July 2002. Some changes are apparent; a pelican crossing now helps pedestrians to cross the road, and St Thomas Square has been closed to traffic. Visible in both photographs is the sign of the Vine Inn on the corner of Holyrood Street; this hostelry dates back to the late 18th century, but its mock Tudor appearance is comparatively modern, dating from a rebuild during the 1930s. In the right foreground what was Lennards' shop is now a Specsavers optician, although the former name is still carried at roof level. On the other side of the entrance to St Thomas Square notice the new premises, built in a traditional style and occupied by the Laura Ashley shop. This company had its origins in a home industry started by Laura Ashley and her husband in 1953. The enterprise grew rapidly, and was soon supplying such famous shops as Fortnum & Mason and Harrods. The first of the Laura Ashley shops was opened in 1968, and from that first outlet in London the retail business grew to over 500 shops around the world. Sadly Laura Ashley herself died in 1985 at the age of 60 as the result of injuries sustained in an accident. *Isle of Wight Record Office/CH*

THE OLD GRAMMAR SCHOOL: This building dates from 1619 and is of particular historical interest in that Charles I was lodged here for a period in 1648. Brought from Carisbrooke Castle, where he had been imprisoned, he stayed here while negotiating with the Parliamentary Commissioners. These meetings resulted in the 1648 Treaty of Newport; this proved abortive, however, and Charles I was taken to London where he was tried and executed in 1649. The building reverted to its original use as a school in that year, and was obliged to accept at least 20 free scholars and permitted to take other day scholars and boarders. Subsequently many generations of youngsters received a good education here; the building was finally taken out of use as a school in 1963. Five years later it became Newport Youth Centre. When the building had been a school there were occasional reports of strange noises being heard in the room once occupied by Charles I, but these were dismissed as adolescent pranks. These stories resurfaced after the building became a youth centre, and a number of young people and youth leaders reported hearing unusual sounds or suddenly feeling very cold in the room. Around the same

period, people passing the building late at night when the centre was closed and locked occasionally reported seeing figures moving around in the first floor room by what appeared to be flickering candlelight. It would be interesting to know if these latter 'manifestations' had coincided with special late licences at any of the local hostelries – or perhaps with unofficial 'ghost hunts' by some of the more adventurous young people! These photographs, taken around 1890 and on Saturday 24 August 2002, illustrate this historic building. *Isle of Wight Record Office/CH*

THE BLUE SCHOOL FOR GIRLS was established at 10 Lugley Street in 1761. It was founded to provide 'for the education, board and clothing of 20 poor girls of Newport', with the intention 'to instruct the children in the duties of servants, and endeavour to make them good Christians and useful subjects'. When a girl left the school to go into service she was given appropriate clothing and a Bible; a further award of £1 was given at the end of the year, provided she remained in service. The school was moved to Crocker Street in the late 19th century, and continued in being until 1907.

These photographs show the original premises in Lugley Street. The 'past' view dates from around 1970, while the 'present' photograph was taken on Saturday 6 July 2002. It will be seen that restoration and refurbishment work has been carried out in the 32 years that separate the two photographs – notice especially the ground-floor windows. In 2002 the building is the Watchbell House Natural Therapy Centre, but carries a small plaque to remind passers-by of its former use. *Isle of Wight Record Office/CH*

MEW LANGTON BREWERY/ MALTHOUSE COURT: It is known that the Mew family were brewing beer in Crocker Street during the 17th century, and by the end of the 18th century a number of inns had been brought together under the name of Mew & Company. The Company thrived, and in 1850 was granted a Royal Warrant to supply Queen Victoria when she was at Osborne House. During the 1870s Walter Langton invested £20,000 into the business, and the title of the undertaking became Mew Langton & Company. Part of their premises in Crocker Street is seen in the 'past' photograph, which dates from around 1960. The Company continued in the hands of the Mew and Langton families until 1965, when it was merged with Strong's of Romsey, Hampshire. Strong's in turn was taken over by Whitbread in 1969, and brewing at Newport ceased in 1972. Happily these rather attractive buildings remain, now tastefully converted into residential accommodation and known as Malthouse Court. The 'present' photograph was taken on Saturday 24 August 2002. *Isle of Wight Record Office/CH*

THE SUN INN on the corner of Holyrood Street and Lugley Street dates back to the 18th Century, and in its early years was a focal point in Newport's social life. Often the location for a grand supper or an elegant ball, it is recorded that in 1790 the then Duke of Gloucester stayed here. The 'past' photograph shows the Sun Inn during the mid-1970s; the mock-Tudor beams and the leaded windows are in fact a 20th-century modification, dating from a refurbishment in the mid-1930s. The Sun closed as a public house in 1978 and subsequently became a delicatessen; as can be seen in the 'present' photograph, taken on Saturday 6 July 2002, it is now the Andrew Ross Hair Studio. The public conveniences just seen in the right foreground of the 'past' photograph have been demolished. In the background of both views is the tower of the Parish Church of St Thomas, affectionately regarded by many as the Isle of Wight's cathedral. This is, in fact, the second church building dedicated to St Thomas to occupy this site. The earlier building dated from the late 12th century, but was demolished in 1854. The first services in the present building were held on Sunday 21 December 1857. Inside the church the Foster and Andrews organ dates from the mid-1870s, being rebuilt in 1926 and the late 1950s. *Isle of Wight Record Office/CH*

QUAY STREET: The origins of Newport go back to the 12th century, when this area on the tidal River Medina at the confluence of the Lukely Brook was established as a port for nearby Carisbrooke – then the most important settlement on the Island. The early development of the town took place in the area between the present High Street and the Quay, and a map of Newport produced in 1611 shows Quay Street following its present alignment and lined by houses.

By the time the 'past' photograph was taken around 1970, part of this side of Quay Street had long been a carrier's depot, occupied by the local firm of Crouchers Limited and by British Road Services. The photograph illustrates a street scene that would have been little changed for decades. The 'present' photograph, taken on Saturday 6 July 2002, shows how this side of Quay Street has been transformed, with the court building taking the place of the old haulage depot. Two of the houses on the left remain, as does the old street name sign above the front door of the first house. *Isle of Wight Record Office/CH*

THE DOLPHIN INN dates from 1758, and was among the older public houses on the Island. Sadly it closed as an inn during 1970, but fortunately the building survives; the exterior is little changed and even the name 'Dolphin' has been preserved on the Sea Street frontage more than 32 years after the hostelry's closure.

These photographs date from around 1970 and Saturday 6 July 2002. Looking in this direction the scene has changed comparatively little over the years – compare with the changes to the other side of Quay Street, out of sight to the left of these photographs and illustrated opposite. The filled-in window spaces on the upper floors of the 'Dolphin' building will be noted. This was a result of the Window Tax, first imposed in 1696 to replace the Hearth Tax, and which was increased during the 18th century. However, the measure was unsatisfactory because in many instances windows were filled in or buildings were constructed in ways to avoid the tax. From 1823 the Window Tax was reduced, and it was abolished in 1851. *Isle of Wight Record Office/CH*

This page THE GUILDHALL was designed by John Nash. The building dates from 1814, but the clock tower on the right-hand corner was added in 1887 to commemorate the Golden Jubilee of Queen Victoria. These photographs were taken in the early 1970s and on Saturday 6 July 2002. At the time of the 'past' photograph traffic could still pass this way from St Thomas Square to the High Street. Three products of the British Motor Corporation, an Allegro, a Traveller and a Maxi – all typical vehicles of that era – will be noted. St Thomas Square has now been pedestrianised; contrasting with the earlier view, no motor cars are visible in the 2002 photograph, although the High Street is still normally very busy with traffic. The Guildhall proclaims its role as a Tourist Information Centre and Museum, and the boxes of plants at first floor level are a welcome addition.

The pedestrianisation of St Thomas Square has enabled the 'One Way' traffic sign to be replaced by a useful finger post to help visiting pedestrians find their way around the town. *Isle of Wight Record Office/CH*

Opposite page COPPINS BRIDGE: It is difficult to believe that these two photographs were taken from the same spot. However, the location can be fixed by the house partly visible to the left of the central support of the viaduct in the 'past' photograph, which can be seen to the left of the trees in the centre of the 'present' view. The 'past' photograph dates from 1960, when road traffic still used Coppins Bridge. The girder viaduct dated from 1920, and had replaced an earlier structure on the same site; it carried the railway line from Newport to Sandown. This closed in February 1956, and four years later we see the viaduct being taken down. I wonder what a present-day Health & Safety Officer would make of passers-by being allowed to stand so close to major demolition work! Part of the road bridge parapet survives in the left foreground of the 'present' photograph, taken in the winter sunshine at midday on Saturday 18 January 2003. A large gyratory system now handles traffic at this point, resulting in Coppins Bridge being used by pedestrians only, while all traces of the railway have completely disappeared. *Isle of Wight Record Office/CH*

SNOOK'S HILL is believed to have taken its name from a local blacksmith who had his forge here during the early 19th century. The 'past' photograph dates from 1976, and the building seen on the left opened as the Victoria Inn during the 1880s. It closed as a public house in the late 1920s, but subsequently the premises were used as a shop and as a hairdressing salon. Together with Hunter & Coombes Marine and Engineering Factors, it was subsequently demolished to facilitate the widening and realignment of Snook's Hill to ease the flow of vehicles on to the gyratory system at Coppins Bridge. The need for this is illustrated by the amount of traffic seen in the 'present' photograph, taken during the late afternoon of Saturday 24 August 2002. The view from this point has changed completely in the 26 years that separate the two photographs, but even with the gyratory system there is still congestion here. *Isle of Wight Record Office/CH*

Cowes

COWES STATION: The first section of railway on the Isle of Wight was the line between Cowes and Newport, which opened on 16 June 1862. The station at Cowes was located on a hillside, and passengers entered by means of a stairway from the corner of Terminus Road and Carvel Lane, as seen in the 'past' photograph, which dates from the early 1960s. In common with many other stations, the Southern Railway signage has survived well into the era of state ownership. The building seen here dated from 1891 and had a pleasant atmosphere; the green and light stone-coloured paintwork was attractive, while inside the building the concourse often had hanging baskets of flowers.

The station closed on 21 February 1966, and the site looks very different in 2002. A Co-op supermarket has been built on the area formerly occupied by the platforms, Carvel Lane has been widened, and a bus terminus has been provided where the station buildings once stood. The bottom of the stairway seen in the 'past' photograph was at a point in front of the bus in the modern view. As can be seen, this location is still an important focal point in the local transport network, and on Saturday 12 October 2002 'Route Rouge'-branded Leyland Olympian TIL 6714, new in November 1989, prepares to depart with the 1.15pm Service 3B to Sandown. *Isle of Wight Record Office/CH*

COWES OLD STATION: After closure in February 1966, Cowes Station survived virtually intact for several years, finally being demolished in 1973. The 'past' photograph was taken from near Granville Bridge in the mid-1970s and looks towards the site of the old station, with the remains of the coal yard on the left. The 'present' photograph was taken from as near as possible to the same point on Saturday 20 July 2002, and shows how this site has been developed for residential use. The location can be fixed by the roof-line of the row of older houses in the centre of both views. Also visible in both photographs is the Roman Catholic Church of St Thomas of Canterbury. The work of building this church started in May 1796, and the first Mass was offered in the building on Trinity Sunday, 11 June 1797. The cost of construction was met by a Mrs Elizabeth Heneage, who five years earlier had also established a Roman Catholic Church in Newport; these were, in fact, among the earliest Roman Catholic churches permitted to be built after the Reformation. The exterior of this church in Cowes has changed very little in the 205 years it has been on this site; the interior is very beautiful, and well worth seeing. *Isle of Wight Record Office/CH*

TERMINUS ROAD in Cowes leads uphill beside the site of the old station towards Northwood Park, and is seen here in the mid-1970s and on Saturday 20 July 2002. The mixture of housing styles on the right-hand side of the road will be noticed in both views; the long block of maisonettes dates from the 1960s. On the left it will be seen that the coal yard and other buildings formerly associated with the railway have in the 2002 photograph been demolished and replaced by residential development with beautifully kept grounds. The small building seen in the centre background of both photographs is a block of public conveniences at one of the entrances to Northwood Park. Northwood House was built for the Ward family in 1838, who presented the house and grounds to the people of Cowes in 1929. The grounds, which include various species of trees from around the world, became a public park, while the house was for many years used as local government offices. The slight realignment of the street and pavements in Terminus Road gives the general scene a more tidy appearance in 2002. *Isle of Wight Record Office/CH*

FOUNTAIN PIER: Records of a steam packet service between Fountain Pier and Southampton go back to the 1820s, when the crossing could be made for the sum of 1 shilling. The ferry service was operated by the Ward family's Isle of Wight Steam Packet Company, which in 1861 was amalgamated with another undertaking to form the Southampton, Isle of Wight & South of England Royal Mail Steam Packet Company, better known as Red Funnel, under which name the service still operates in 2002. The first photograph dates from around 1890 and shows the improved entrance building to the pier, completed in 1874. Notice the horse-drawn carriage waiting to provide an onward connection for passengers from the ferry.

The second photograph dates from around 1980. At that time the Red Funnel car ferries between East Cowes and Southampton still called here and there was also a high-speed hydrofoil service to Southampton for foot passengers. Pedestrian access to the hydrofoils can be seen on the left, while motorists are waiting for the ferry, which they will board by means of the slipway seen on the right. Notice the Arcade on the left.

The third photograph was taken from the same location around 22 years later, on Thursday 17 October 2002. The car ferries no longer call here, but an improved terminal for foot passengers using the high-speed service was opened in May 1990, including a new ticket office and a more spacious waiting area. Few changes are apparent to the Arcade on the left, but the turf accountant is now controlled by Ladbrokes while the newsagent now advertises *The Observer* rather than the Express Group! Consistent with the first photograph is the Southern Vectis bus waiting to depart for Newport at 1.25pm, thus providing an onward connection for passengers arriving on the ferry from Southampton. *Isle of Wight Record Office (2)/CH*

HIGH STREET: A period of just over 28 years separates these views of Cowes High Street, which are taken looking north from the entrance to Fountain Pier. The 'past' photograph was taken on 2 February 1974 and shows the street still in use by motor traffic; the section north of Fountain Pier – already one-way southbound only – was pedestrianised shortly afterwards. In 1974 the Red Funnel Car Ferry and Passenger Hydrofoil to Southampton departed from Fountain Pier; in 2002 the car ferry runs from East Cowes only, while Fountain Pier is linked to Southampton by the Red Jet high-speed service – notice the change to the sign on the right.

The 'present' photograph was taken on Saturday 20 July 2002. The more people-friendly atmosphere of the pedestrianised street is immediately apparent in this view taken at lunchtime on a pleasant summer day. Many of the shops cater for the holidaymaker or yachting enthusiast, and the whole area has a very pleasant and safe aspect. However, if we turn the clock back to the old days of Cowes as a port, the area then had a less savoury reputation. Sun Hill, a turning on the left just out of sight in the background of the photographs, is said to have contained a brothel known as 'Shanghai Lil's' – so-called because many men were apparently shanghaied for service at sea from there. *Isle of Wight Record Office/CH*

THE PARADE AND ROYAL YACHT SQUADRON: Cowes is arguably the most famous yachting resort in Great Britain, and Cowes Week, held every August, is certainly the premier yachting occasion. The history of yachting at Cowes goes back to 1815 when a group of gentlemen met at the Thatched House Tavern in St James Street, London. They decided to form a club for those interested in sea yachting, known initially as the Yacht Club. After King George IV was elected a member it became the Royal Yacht Club and by the mid-1820s was based at The Parade in Cowes – in the building that can be seen as the Gloster Hotel in the 'past' photograph. In 1833 the Club's title was changed to the Royal Yacht Squadron, and in 1856 it moved across the road to Cowes Castle, which can be seen in the right background of both photographs. Parts of this building date back to 1539, constructed on the orders of Henry VIII; in 2002 it is still the headquarters of the Royal Yacht Squadron. When the 'past' photograph

was taken on 11 August 1973 the weather was clearly rather inclement – and the Ford Transit police van is now quite a period piece! The weather was much nicer on Saturday 20 July 2002 when the 'present' photograph was taken. The most noticeable change is that the Gloster Hotel has been replaced by apartments; notice also the 'heritage'-style street lighting when compared with the earlier view. The building on the extreme left has survived with few changes in the 29 years that separate the two photographs. This is the premises of the Royal London Yacht Club, which was founded at The Coal Hole Tavern in Strand, London, in 1836, and which moved to Cowes in 1882. *Isle of Wight Record Office/CH*

THE PARADE AND VICTORIA PIER: These photographs were taken from the foot of Castle Hill, Cowes, during the 1930s and on Thursday 17 October 2002. The views look south-east along The Parade, with Spring Hill, East Cowes, visible across the water in the background. In general the scene is readily recognisable, but one feature is missing from the modern view. In the 'past' photograph Victoria Pier can be seen running from the further end of The Parade to its substantial pier head, complete with pavilion. The pier opened in 1902, and the pavilion was provided a few years later. It soon became a very popular amenity, with excursion steamers calling and nightly entertainment in the pavilion in season. This all came to an end with the Second World War, when the pier was taken over by the Navy. At the end of hostilities the structure was found to be in a very poor state, and no funding was available for repairs. The pavilion was demolished in 1951, but the pier itself remained derelict until it was dismantled in 1961. The Parade, with its attractive stone balustrade along the seaward side, dates from around 1900, and has changed little in the 70 or so years that separate the two photographs. *Isle of Wight Record Office/CH*

HOLY TRINITY CHURCH is close to the Royal Yacht Squadron, and looks across Queens Road and the Esplanade to the sea at the western edge of the town. Designed by William Bramble, the nave is nearly 90 feet long, and the church was consecrated by the Bishop of Winchester in 1832. The clock was installed in the tower to commemorate the Coronation of Queen Victoria in 1837. The chancel (not visible in these views) was added in 1862.

The photographs were taken from Queens Road in the late 1950s and on Saturday 20 July 2002. Unsurprisingly there have been few visible exterior changes to this beautiful church. Inside the building, the Beaverbrook Foundation paid for the organ to be rebuilt in 1989 as a memorial to the late Sir Max Aitken.

The rather attractive building to the right of the church in the 'past' view was part of Solent House School, which has now been replaced by a terrace of modern homes. *Isle of Wight Record Office/CH*

THE GREEN: In the mid 19th century a Mr George Stephenson, nephew of the George Stephenson who built the famous railway locomotive *Rocket*, lived at Grantham House (now demolished and replaced by the Grantham Court apartments) in Cowes. In 1863 he purchased the adjacent two acres of grassland, and gave it to the people of Cowes to commemorate the marriage of the then Prince of Wales to Princess Alexandra of Denmark. The kindly Mr Stephenson also donated £50 to pay for a celebratory meal to be provided for the poorer people of Cowes, so that they too would remember the Royal occasion with pleasure.

These photographs show The Green, looking west, with the Esplanade and shingle beach. The 'past' view dates from around 1923 and we can see a large number of people, dressed in the fashions of the time, enjoying this amenity. The location is easily recognised in the 'present' photograph, taken during the afternoon of Saturday 20 July 2002. Although fewer people can be seen, it is nonetheless pleasing to see that the area is still enjoyed by all age groups; the more casual approach to sartorial matters in 2002 will be noted. Notice also the shelters beside the Esplanade. Between two of these shelters can be found a very interesting feature – a Victorian drinking fountain. This has a delightful ornate iron framework that includes a quotation from St John's Gospel, Chapter 4, verses 13 and 14: 'Whosoever drinketh of this water shall thirst again, but whosoever drinketh of the water I shall give him shall never thirst.' *Isle of Wight Record Office/CH*

GURNARD BEACH: The gently shelving sand and shingle beach at Gurnard is seen in the 'past' photograph around 1950. In 1926 the then Prince of Wales opened Princes Esplanade, which provides a coast road between Cowes and Gurnard, but this takes a slightly more inland course at this point, following the line of buildings seen in the centre background of both photographs. Between the road and the beach there is a pleasant grassed area, the beach huts and a pedestrian promenade, making this an ideal location for family bathing as well as for boating. Lots of people can be seen enjoying this pleasant spot in the 'past' view.

The 'present' photograph was taken during the late afternoon of Saturday 20 July 2002. The scene is little changed despite the 52 years that separate the photographs. Both the beach huts and the buildings in the background are readily recognisable. The slipway in the foreground has lost its seaward extension, and in place of the moored boats we see a small yacht on a road trailer, no doubt about to be towed away for storage in the owner's garden. *Isle of Wight Record Office/CH*

GURNARD HOTEL AND POST OFFICE: These photographs were taken at the junction of Worsley Road and Church Road in Gurnard. The 'past' photograph dates from around 1920, and part of the Gurnard Hotel can be seen on the right. This closed in the late 1970s and was demolished a few years later. Much of the site is now occupied by Bucklers View, elderly people's dwellings, opened in 1986, which is set further back from the road, and is therefore out of sight to the right of the 'present' photograph, taken on Saturday 20 July 2002. The crescent-shaped walled enclosures seen in the foreground contain bench seats, which are no doubt appreciated by local residents.

The Post Office, seen on the left of the 'past' view, can be recognised in the 2002 photograph, but the building has been converted for residential use, the Post Office itself having been moved to a newer building next door. Notice the delightful horse-drawn delivery van for Lyons Tea in the centre of the 'past' photograph. *Isle of Wight Record Office/CH*

THE HOVERCRAFT HANGER: This distinctive building, with its huge Union Jack emblem painted on the doors, is a well-known landmark for people coming to the Isle of Wight via Cowes. The firm of S. E. Saunders Limited had been set up in East Cowes in 1908, and specialised in the construction of lightweight, high-speed boats. In 1928 the famous partnership of Saunders-Roe was established, a company that became particularly associated with seaplanes and flying boats. However, the main claim to fame for Saunders-Roe was to come during the 1960s. The inventor Sir Christopher Cockerell had proved in the early 1950s that it was possible to travel on a cushion of air, and in 1959 the National Research & Development Corporation commissioned Saunders-Roe to build the first manned hovercraft, the SRN 1. In 1964 the Company opened the first commercial hovercraft production line in the world here at East Cowes. In 1965 SRN 5 hovercraft from this factory started the service between Ryde and Portsmouth; a service from Ryde still operates and now uses AP1-88 hovercraft – see also page 95. Saunders-Roe was taken over by Westland Aircraft in the early 1960s, and in 1966 the Company acquired the hovercraft interests of Vickers, so forming the British Hovercraft Corporation.

The 'past' view dates from the late 1970s, and shows the hovercraft hanger with the large Union Jack logo that was originally applied to mark the Silver Jubilee of Queen Elizabeth II in 1977. As can be seen from the 'present' photograph, taken on Saturday 20 July 2002, it is still in place 25 years later! (No, it was not a special re-application for the Golden Jubilee!) Since 1994 the Company has been known as GKN Westland Aerospace Limited, and sadly hovercraft are no longer built here. Nonetheless the Company still undertakes an important role supplying components and engineering services to the aviation industry. *Isle of Wight Record Office/CH*

FLOATING BRIDGE: The chain ferry or floating bridge between Cowes and East Cowes commenced operation in November 1859. The 'past' photograph dates from around 1898 and shows the 1896 ferry vessel on the East Cowes side of the crossing. Built by White's of Cowes at a cost of £2,772, this craft remained with the floating bridge undertaking until 1925, when it was sold to the yacht-designer and boat-builder Uffa Fox. Operation of the floating bridge was taken over by the Urban District Council in 1901, and passed to the Isle of Wight County Council in 1972.

The 'present' photograph was taken on Saturday 20 July 2002 and shows the current ferry loading vehicles at East Cowes. This craft was built by Fairey Marine of East Cowes at a cost of £280,000 and entered service in 1976. In 2002 the floating bridge is still a vital link between East and West Cowes. *Isle of Wight Record Office/CH*

FLOATING BRIDGE: For our second look at the floating bridge we see the ferry on the West Cowes side of the crossing. The 'past' photograph was taken during the 1960/61 winter, and illustrates the flooding that was experienced at that time. The ferry vessel we see here entered service in May 1952, having been built by Bolson's of Poole, Dorset, at a cost of £26,530. A popular feature of this craft was the upper deck for passengers; it also had the capacity for 12 cars. The 1976 replacement ferry can carry 18 cars, but unfortunately does not have upper passenger decks.

The narrow roadway, with the ferry ramp right beside the ticket office, will be noted in the 'past' view. Road widening took place during the summer of 1975; the improved approach to the ferry, together with the

replacement office buildings, can be seen in the 'present' photograph, taken on Saturday 20 July 2002. Tickets are no longer sold from the office buildings; since 1992 pedestrians and cyclists have travelled free, while charges for vehicles are collected on the ferry. *Isle of Wight Record Office/CH*

OSBORNE HOUSE: No exploration of the Isle of Wight would be complete without a visit to Osborne House; probably the Island's best-known attraction. Queen Victoria purchased the Osborne Estate in 1845 with the intention that it should be a country retreat, away from the affairs of state. The present Osborne House was designed by Prince Albert, working closely with the London builder Thomas Cubitt. Most of the house was built between 1845 and 1851, and can be seen in the 'past' photograph, which dates from the late 1880s. One feature that was lacking at Osborne House as originally constructed was a state banqueting hall. This omission was remedied in 1890-91 when the Durbar Wing was added. Queen Victoria had become Empress of India in 1876, and part of the interior of this wing is designed in an Indian style. On the ground floor is the Durbar Room, its name derived from an Indian word for a state reception and used for such functions, while accommodation for Princess Beatrice and her family was provided above. Queen Victoria died at Osborne House on 22 January 1901, and the following year her son, King Edward VII, gave Osborne House to the nation; some rooms were opened to the public in 1904. Areas open to visitors have subsequently been increased in 1954, 1989, 2000 and 2002, and Osborne House is now cared for by English Heritage. An extensive repair and restoration project commenced in 1993, which has included returning the external walls to their original appearance. The 'present' view was taken on Saturday 12 October 2002; note the addition of the Durbar Wing on the right when comparing this with the 'past' photograph. *Isle of Wight Record Office/CH*

Ryde and North East Wight

RYDE ESPLANADE STATION: For many years Southern Vectis rented some railway-owned buildings at Ryde Esplanade Station for use as offices and staff accommodation; bus services departed from a line of roadside shelters. The 'past' photograph was taken around 1960, and shows the Southern Vectis booking office next to the entrance to the railway ticket office. Twelve years after nationalisation the station still sports a large Southern Railway sign, although the poster sites behind the bus shelter have British Railways corporate identity. It is interesting to note that while the main sign highlights both routes from Portsmouth to London, no mention is made of the railway service that then existed to a number of Island destinations. Part of W. H. Smith's ornate canopy can be seen on the left.

Ryde Esplanade Station was rebuilt in the early 1970s, and at that time a purpose-built bus station with eight saw-tooth-style departure stands and layover space for 12 buses was provided. Ryde bus station opened on 25 May 1974. The 'present' photograph, taken on Saturday 19 October 2002, shows the reconstructed Ryde Esplanade Station, which still includes a newsagent and stationer's shop. The bus station is to the right of the 'present' view; two buses can be glimpsed on layover on the extreme right. *Southern Vectis Collection/CH*

RYDE ESPLANADE: These photographs compare the scene looking west along Ryde Esplanade in the early years of the 20th century and on Saturday 21 September 2002. Prominent in the centre background of the 'past' photograph is the Royal Pier Hotel. Dating from the 1820s, this was at one time one of the main hotels in Ryde, but it was bought by the Council and demolished in 1927 as part of a road improvement scheme. The Eagle Hotel, centre left in the 'past' view, closed in 1935, but the building remains, the ground floor being an amusement arcade while the upper stories are in residential use. Beside the Eagle, what used to be the premises of Chaplin & Company, Household Removals and Warehousing, is in 2002 occupied by The Cod Father, purveyor of Traditional Fish & Chips.

On the other side of George Street the Marine Hotel, opened around 1870, survives as a public house but is no longer a hotel. In the left foreground the Royal Esplanade Hotel, dating from 1869, remains a popular place to stay. Plenty of activity can be observed in the 'past' photograph, with horse-drawn vehicles much in evidence. The demise of this form of conveyance also led in due course to the loss of the rather attractive lamp standard with incorporated horse trough, seen in front of the Royal Pier Hotel.

In the 'present' view a motorist has stopped at the zebra crossing that is now needed to help pedestrians cross the road at this point, while buses of various types can be seen in the 1974 Bus Station on the right (see opposite). The 'heritage'-style street lighting installed in recent years is good, and the Esplanade retains a very pleasant atmosphere. *Classic Pictures/CH*

UNION STREET, RYDE, runs downhill from High Street to the Esplanade. These photographs look towards the sea around 1914 and on Saturday 21 September 2002. The general scene, with part of the pier visible in the background, is readily recognisable, and the exteriors of many of the buildings have changed very little. However, at the time of the 'past' photograph the street was definitely for people, and only one early motor car can be seen, while in 2002 the roadway is clearly the domain of the car.

Union Street has one possible claim to fame in song-writing history; in 1960 the licensee of the Bow Bars was a cousin of a certain Paul McCartney, who came down from Merseyside to spend some time in Ryde during that summer. It could be speculated that in the 1965 hit 'Ticket to Ride' he may have had in mind 'Ticket to Ryde'!

Classic Pictures/CH

CROSS STREET, RYDE: Over a hundred years separate these photographs, taken looking east along Cross Street from its junction with Ryde High Street, but most of the buildings can easily be recognised and there is no difficulty in establishing the location. The large building on the corner of George Street in the background of the 'past' photograph, taken around 1900, was a Congregational Church. This building opened for worship on 2 June 1872 and was on the site of an earlier church that had been destroyed by fire in April 1869. As can be seen from the 'present' photograph, taken on Saturday 28 September 2002, the 1872 building has sadly now been demolished and replaced by a furniture store. Notice the fashions and also the variety of conveyances visible in the 'past' photograph. There were fewer people about when I took the 'present' photograph, but just beyond the second bus shelter a battery-powered mobility aid of a type that has become very popular with elderly people in recent years can be seen parked on the pavement. *Classic Pictures/CH*

SEAVIEW PIER opened on 7 June 1881. Designed by a local engineer, Frank Caws, the pier was built on the suspension principle, largely because of the rocky shoreline, which would have presented problems in building a pier by the more conventional method of using numerous piles. The pier head was extended in 1889, and the structure, which was known as the Chain Pier, is seen in the 'past' photograph around 1900.

During the Second World War the pier was taken over by the Navy. Unlike most piers it was not sectioned, but with no maintenance being undertaken for the duration, it was in a very bad state by the end of hostilities. By this time the only suspension pier in England, Seaview Chain Pier was given 'listed' status in 1950, but restoration work had yet to begin when a severe storm in December 1950 virtually destroyed it, the remainder having to be demolished during 1951. This sad end to a remarkable structure does have an amusing sequel. A story, possibly apocryphal, is told of a Government Inspector who came to Seaview in 1970 to check on the safety of the pier – he was apparently surprised to be told that most of it had fallen into the sea almost 20 years earlier! As can be seen in the 'present' photograph, taken on Saturday 28 September 2002, no trace remains of the pier, and the sea wall has been extended in recent years. *Classic Pictures/CH*

ST HELENS is a delightful village with about 1,200 residents, situated close to Bembridge Harbour. One of its most pleasant features is the way that the heart of the village is arranged around a large green, which is still used for organised sport. A very small part of the green can be seen in the foreground of these photographs; when I took the 'present' view during the afternoon of Saturday 28 September 2002 a game of football was taking place – a corner flag can be seen in the right foreground.

When the 'past' photograph was taken in the early years of the 20th century the right-hand end of this terrace in Lower Green Road was the local Post Office; this facility can now be found in Upper Green Road on the other side of the green. The shop seen here served as a Post Office between 1898 and 1924; it was later part of the Isle of Wight Co-operative Society, but was converted for residential use around 1980. In 2002 the location is still easily recognisable. The removal of the climbing plants from the left-hand end has improved the look of the building. Notice also that two chimney stacks have been removed and replaced by outlets from central heating systems. *Classic Pictures/CH*

Opposite page BEMBRIDGE STATION: The branch line from Brading to Bembridge was opened on 27 May 1882. Bembridge Station was close to the shore and some way from the centre of the village, but nonetheless a good train service was provided, and the majority of trains between Ryde and Ventnor that stopped at Brading had a connection to and from Bembridge.

The 'past' photograph dates from around 1952 and shows the branch train ready to depart for Brading hauled by one of the Class 'O2' tank engines, which, named after various Island locations, were so much part of the Isle of Wight railway scene. The locomotive seen here was built in October 1890 and was transferred to the Isle of Wight, where it was given the number 23 and the name *Totland* in April 1925. In August 1955 it became one of the first Isle of Wight 'O2s' to be withdrawn. Some locomotive of this class were in service until the end of steam on the Island in 1967, and sister loco *Calbourne* (No 24) is still active in 2002 on the Isle of Wight Steam Railway at the grand age of 112 years.

Bembridge Station closed on 21 September 1953. The tracks have long gone and the attractive station building has been demolished. Some functional residential blocks stand where the platform used to be, as seen in the 'present' photograph taken on Saturday 21 September 2002, while the cul-de-sac road on part of the old trackbed is called Harbour Strand. In fact, the only clue as to the site's former use is the nearby street that is still called **Station Road**. *Classic Pictures/CH*

Above BRADING OLD TOWN HALL AND CHURCH: These photographs, taken in 1935 and on Saturday 27 July 2002, illustrate how little has changed in 67 years at this attractive location. The old town hall building in the centre of the photographs dates from 1730. At that time Brading was a seaport; a sea wall was built from St Helens to Bembridge and the land to Brading was reclaimed during the second half of the 19th century, but Brading Harbour was navigable for cargo boats until 1881. Brading Corporation was abolished by the Municipal Corporations Act, 1883, but in 1898 the Town Trust was formed to administer the affairs of the Borough. A new town hall was opened in 1902 (see page 45) and the building seen here became a museum.

The Church of St Mary the Virgin can be seen behind the old town hall. Prominent in the photographs is the bell tower and spire, dating from the 13th century. Entry to the church is through the base of the tower, which is open on three sides – an unusual arrangement thought to be shared by only three other churches in England. Inside the church the organ dates from around 1804; located at the east end of the church it was rebuilt by Foster and Andrews of Hull in 1864. During 1978 Colmer Brothers overhauled the organ and moved it to its present position in the nave. Sadly there was a fire, caused by vandals, in the church in November 1989; the organ was subsequently rebuilt by Vectis Organ Services of Wooton Bridge. *Isle of Wight Record Office/CH*

BRADING HIGH STREET: These photographs look north along Brading High Street and were taken around 1912 and on Saturday 27 July 2002. The location is readily recognisable, and it is pleasing to note that there is still a range of shops to provide for the needs of local people. More prosaic signs of the times are the 'pay point' and National Lottery logos displayed by the Londis outlet on the extreme right of the 'present' photograph. The loss of some houses to make room for a car park by the Bugle Inn will also be noted.

Of particular interest is the building in the left foreground of the photographs. Built by William Russell of Yaverland Manor as his town house in 1623, by the end of the 19th century the premises were being used as a Parish Club and Reading Room, and can be seen as such in the 1912 view. In 1914 a tea room and guest house

was established here, run by a Miss Young and a Miss Morris, great-aunts of the present owner, Gill Lee. The establishment passed to Gill's parents in 1953, and Gill took over in 1977. Under Gill's management the building is again used as a reading room and heritage centre as well as a tea room; it has a lovely happy atmosphere and is also reputed to be home to a friendly ghost! I recommend visitors to Brading to call in for delicious coffee and home-made cake and to peruse some of the interesting books in the reading room. *Isle of Wight Record Office/CH*

BRADING BULL RING is a timing point for the Southern Vectis buses passing through the town. The location is seen here around 1930 and on Saturday 27 July 2002. The Londis shop can again be seen on the right, and fixes the location in relation to the photographs opposite.

Notice the delightful finger post and street lamp in the 1930 photograph. Many years previously a bull ring was fixed to the ground here and was used to tether bulls, which were then taunted by specially trained dogs prior to being slaughtered. Much more traffic is evident in the 2002 photograph; the ornate street lamp has gone (replaced by a plain but functional modern equivalent) and instead of the friendly finger post there is a less welcome warning of the ubiquitous speed camera!

To the left of the photographs can be seen the new town hall, which was built in 1902 and replaced the building illustrated on page 43. The bus stop used by services travelling towards Ryde is seen in the 'present' photograph, and the provision of a large, well-designed shelter for waiting passengers will be noted. *Isle of Wight Record Office/CH*

BRADING STATION opened with the section of railway from Ryde (St John's Road) to Shanklin on 23 August 1864. In 1882 it became the junction for the branch to Bembridge (see also page 42). Passenger services on the Bembridge branch ceased in September 1953, but part of the branch line between Brading and St Helens remained in railway use until November 1957. The line from Ryde to Shanklin was electrified in March 1967. These photographs of Brading station are looking towards Ryde and were taken in 1985 and on Saturday 27 July 2002. Trains for Bembridge had used the platform on the extreme right of the photographs – long disused in both views. In 1985 there was still double track through the station, with both platforms and the signal box in use. Despite being served by electric trains the station was still gas-lit at that time, and it has to be said that the general appearance of the premises, complete with football-inspired graffiti, was a little shabby.

Electric lighting was installed in October 1986; fortunately care was taken to provide fittings in a similar style to the gas lamps being replaced, as can be seen in the 'present' photograph. The line was singled in October 1988, resulting in the closure of the signal box, although that structure, the now disused island platform buildings and the footbridge remain in place. However, although nature is fast reclaiming the area once used by trains to Bembridge, the station, complete with its 'Stagecoach Island Line' corporate identity, has a very pleasant atmosphere in 2002. *Isle of Wight Record Office/CH*

South East and South Wight

YAVERLAND MANOR AND CHURCH: Completed around 1620, Yaverland Manor is an excellent example of an early Jacobean house. Prior to its construction, a house dating from the early 12th century had stood here. The Church of St John the Baptist, seen to the left of the house in the photographs, also has its origins in the 12th century, having been built around 1150 as a chapel for the Lords of the Manor of Yaverland. The church was heavily 'restored' in 1889; the chancel was lengthened, a north aisle added and the building given a new roof incorporating a spirelet. The 'restored' church was re-consecrated on Tuesday 9 July 1889 and was described at the time by the Bishop of Guildford as 'a little gem of a church'. When I visited 113 years later, a poem in the church porch by American poet E. E. Cummings spoke of 'A little church ... at peace with nature', and that very much summed up the atmosphere on that Saturday morning, with no other humans or traffic in sight or earshot.

When the 'past' photograph was taken in 1905 there was a good view of the church and the house from the road. The 'present' photograph, taken on Saturday 7 September 2002, illustrates that much of the view is now obliterated by a high, dense hedge. Behind this obstruction very little has changed in the 97 years that separate the two photographs, and Yaverland remains a delightful spot. *Isle of Wight Record Office/CH*

Opposite page THE CHURCH OF ST JOHN THE EVANGELIST, SANDOWN was consecrated in 1881. Designed by C. Luck of London, the church is built of local stone in the Victorian Gothic style, and an attractive spirelet graces the roof. The 'past' photograph was taken around 1890, and shows this lovely church when less than ten years old; at that time it stood in a relatively open situation. In comparison, the 'present' view, taken on Saturday 27 July 2002, shows the church in a much more urban setting. When I visited a flower festival was taking place, with the interior of the church beautifully decorated.

The church itself looks very little changed over the 122 years that separate the photographs. Much of the stained glass in the lower windows was put in during the late 19th and early 20th centuries. Inside the church the Father Willis organ was relocated to the west gallery during the 1960s; for acoustic reasons the choir is now positioned at the front of the nave rather than in the chancel. *Isle of Wight Record Office/CH*

Above PORTER'S SHOP/LADIES REALM, SANDOWN: For many years one of the most distinctive buildings in Sandown High Street was Porter's shop on the corner of Wilkes Road. It is seen in the 'past' photograph around 1930, with the main part of the premises used as an art shop, and a smaller tobacconist at the north end of the building in the High Street. The main part of the building was later a fancy goods and toy shop. The current owners bought the building from Porter's in 1960, and at first continued to run the establishment as two shops, with clothing in the main section and a wool shop in the former tobacconist. The structural condition of the exterior walls had deteriorated over the years and in 1970 extensive renovation had to be carried out, resulting in the transformation of the building to its present-day appearance. The two shop units were made into one, and the entrance was moved to its current corner position. The 'present' view shows this still very interesting building on Saturday 27 July 2002. *Isle of Wight Record Office/CH*

SHANKLIN BUS STATION: When Southern Vectis took over the coach operations of H. G. Eames in July 1937, the deal included Eames's garage in Carter Avenue, Shanklin. Over the next couple of years the garage accommodation at this site was extended, and a booking hall and staff offices were opened in 1939. The premises were twice damaged by bombing during the Second World War, one of the raids resulting in the tragic death of a conductress. Also bombed during the war was the adjacent Gloster Hotel, and in the mid-1950s work commenced to provide a bus station on the cleared site. This opened in June 1956, with the hard standing being further extended in 1960. The 'past' photograph shows the bus station at this time, with the 1939 offices on the right and the garage to the rear sporting a large map of the Island on its wall. A Bedford coach is laying over against the railings, while a number of passengers queue at one of the bus departure stands. The 1939 travel office was refurbished when the bus station opened, and was again modernised early in 1979.

By the end of 1983 Southern Vectis needed to make a number of economy measures, and it was announced that these premises at Shanklin would be disposed of. The depot closed in April 1984, although the bus station continued in use until the autumn of that year when services were moved to roadside stands, one of which can be seen in the 'present' photograph, taken on Saturday 19 October 2002. A Somerfield supermarket, with its associated car park, now occupies the site, and a casual visitor would have no indication that 20 years previously there had been a bus station here. *Southern Vectis Collection/CH*

REGENT STREET, SHANKLIN: For a number of years Southern Vectis rented a shop on the corner of Regent Street and Clarendon Road in Shanklin for use as a booking office. The 'past' photograph shows the premises around 1960 and is a delightful period piece, epitomising the atmosphere of the time. Notice the fashions worn by the couple on the right and the almost knee-length shorts worn by the two boys looking in the shop window on the left. Also worthy of note is the life-size cut-out of a bathing beauty used to advertise Ilford films. In the booking office the large artwork for the whole-day 'Round the Island' tour seems to be supported on an easel. Just look at the plethora of direction signs – pointing the way to the Coach and Bus Station, the Lift, the Post Office, Public Lavatories and the Information Bureau.

This scene can be compared with the 'present' photograph, taken on Saturday 19 October 2002. When no longer required by Southern Vectis the shop became a bakery, later becoming Island Glass, and since 1998 has been Isle of Wight Jewellers. The door has been moved to the corner section and part of the premises in Clarendon Road has become a luggage shop. The shops to the left and right are respectively still a chemist and a barber. It can be seen that the habit of window shopping is still alive and well! The street lamp, pillar box, shop canopy and direction signs have gone, but note that the old Clarendon Road street nameplate survives on the wall above the new shop doorway.
Southern Vectis Collection/CH

HIGH STREET, SHANKLIN: These photographs compare the scene looking north along Shanklin High Street in the 1920s and on Saturday 28 September 2002. Shanklin United Reform Church is prominent in the background of both views. This is, in fact, the third church building to occupy the location. In 1841 the Carter Estate had granted a 99-year lease on this piece of land so that a Nonconformist chapel could be erected. A lease for 999 years was granted in 1852, so a second, larger church building was constructed and opened on 27 April 1853. This building was in turn replaced by the present church. The clock tower includes a foundation stone laid on 26 October 1882 and the building was opened for worship on 21 August 1883. Close study of the photographs will reveal differences in the tower. In 1947 the top half of the tower was found to be unsafe, having been affected by bombing in the area during the Second World War, and was therefore demolished. Rebuilding was completed in 1954, and the extent of the new construction can easily be seen in the 2002 photograph. In the left foreground what was the National Provincial Bank is now the National Westminster, but with few changes to the exterior of the building. The scene is readily recognisable after a gap of almost 80 years, and Shanklin High Street remains a very pleasant place to stroll. *Classic Pictures/CH*

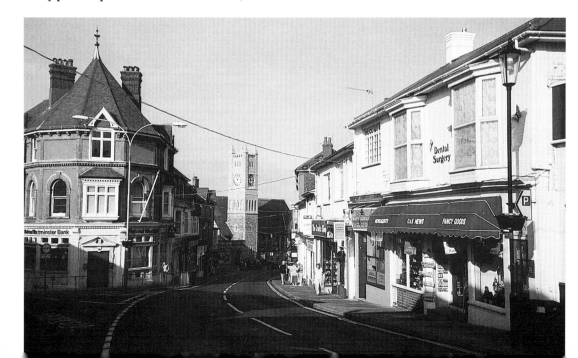

WROXALL: Mentioned in the Domesday Book, Wroxall is situated roughly midway between Shanklin and Ventnor. The name of the village is of interest: 'Wroc' is an old word for a buzzard, and it is possible that the name originally meant a place where buzzards nested. A number of the houses along the main street date from the 1860s when the railway was extended through to Ventnor. The line was truncated at Shanklin in April 1966, resulting in the closure of Wroxall Station, but in 2002 the street in the centre of the photographs is still called Station Road. The 'past' photograph was taken on 8 September 1973 and shows the Co-operative Society stores on the corner of Station Road and the High Street; this shop had previously been known as the Supply Stores and was at one time the Wroxall Bakery. In the 'present' view, taken on Saturday 3 August 2002, it can be seen that this shop has been demolished to give a better alignment and elevation to the road junction. Wroxall Newsagents, the next shop in Station Road, remains – a careful study of the first-floor windows and the house doorways between the two shops illustrates where the building has been divided. Notice the new development on the left of Station Road. In the background a Southern Vectis bus picks up passengers at Wroxall Community Centre for the 1255 departure for Ventnor. *Isle of Wight Record Office/CH*

ST BONIFACE OLD CHURCH, BONCHURCH, near Ventnor, dates from 1070. The windows are later, and the porch and bell-cot were added in the 18th century. These photographs, showing the south side of the church, were taken around 1890 and on Saturday 3 August 2002.

By the 1840s Bonchurch was expanding, and this tiny church was becoming inadequate for the growing population. Extending the building was considered, and it was even suggested that this lovely little church should be pulled down, a larger replacement being provided in the same location. In the event a new church building was constructed on another site nearby and consecrated as the parish church in 1848. Services are still held in the old church on St Boniface Day (5 June) and on Sunday evenings during the summer months.

Prominent in the arrangements for building the new church was Captain Swinburne. His son, Algernon Charles, was baptised in the old church in 1842, but later became an atheist (and a well-known poet). H. de Vere Stacpoole, a ship's doctor and writer, lived at Bonchurch from 1930 until his death in 1951. Best known for his novel *The Blue Lagoon* (and perhaps even better known for the filmed version starring Brooke Shields), his interesting booklet of 'Historical Notes on St Boniface Old Church' is still available from the church. *Isle of Wight Record Office/CH*

SPRING HILL, VENTNOR, was at one time the main road leading into the town centre, and some of the older buildings in the town were found here. In 1838 Ventnor was a fishing village with a population of around 350; by 1870 it had become a noted resort with more than 5,000 inhabitants. Effectively built on a series of terraces that zigzag their way down to the seafront, part of the charm of Ventnor is that it was developed piecemeal rather than built to a plan, so there is a variety of designs and types of buildings. These photographs were taken looking north up Spring Hill from close to its junction with Ventnor High Street around 1890 and on Saturday 3 August 2002. What had been 'The Carisbrooke Dining & Tea Rooms' in the 1890 photograph was demolished, together with the other buildings in the right foreground, in 1973. Part of this land, as can be seen in the 2002 view, is a pleasant public garden – the remainder forms part of a car park. The two buildings on the left-hand side of the road in the background of the 1890 view can still be recognised in the modern photograph, although the dormer window in the roof of the first house has been extended. *Isle of Wight Record Office/CH*

PIER STREET BUS GARAGE, VENTNOR: In June 1956 Southern Vectis acquired the old-established business of Nash's Luxury Coaches of Ventnor. As well as five coaches (see also page 86) the deal also included Nash's coach station in Pier Street, Ventnor. The 'past' photograph dates from around 1960 and shows the former Nash premises, which provided parking space for six coaches, bearing Southern Vectis corporate identity but structurally little changed from their days in Nash ownership. The building to the left of the bus garage was bought by Southern Vectis in 1958 and was let as the Tropicana Coffee Bar – judging by the bottles of milk on the doorstep the 1960 view was taken early in the day!

Extensive works were soon to be undertaken to enlarge the garage and make it suitable for double-deck buses, the rebuilt premises coming into use in 1962. Sadly this resulted in the demise of the Coffee Bar. Daylight was

fading at 3.30pm on Saturday 18 January 2003 when I took the 'present' photograph. Island Explorer-liveried Volvo Olympian M750 HDL, new in March 1995, had just parked in the garage, having operated the 2.10pm Service 7 journey from Ryde. To the right of the bus garage the Rose Inn survives, but the shop on the left is now a hairdressing salon. Notice the old-style direction signs attached to the street lamp in the 'past' photograph. *Southern Vectis Collection/CH*

VENTNOR PIER: These photographs date from around 1925 and Saturday 3 August 2002, and compare the scene looking east along the Esplanade at Ventnor. A number of buildings in the town will be recognised in both views. Sadly the Metropole Hotel, prominent on the Esplanade, was closed and boarded up when the 2002 photograph was taken.

Part of Ventnor Pier can be seen in the 1925 view. This was, in fact, the third pier to have been built in that location, two previous piers having been destroyed by heavy seas after very short lives. The Royal Victoria Pier seen here was built in 1885-7. A theatre was provided at the pier head (out of sight to the right of the 'past' photograph) in 1906, and the pier was much used by excursion steamers. Breached as an anti-invasion measure during the Second World War, reconstruction work started in 1950. By that time a complete rebuild was needed, and at its official opening on 28 May 1955 it was described as 'a new pier ... the most modern in Britain'. For a while the pier enjoyed another halcyon period, but changes in holiday habits led to a reversal in fortunes, and the excursion steamers had largely ceased to call by the end of the 1960s. In 1985 a fire at the shore end of the pier caused severe damage; the cost of restoration was prohibitive, and the structure was eventually demolished in 1993. *Isle of Wight Record Office/CH*

THE SPYGLASS INN, VENTNOR, is situated at the western end of the beach. Dating from around 1830, it is one of Ventnor's earlier buildings, and can be seen above the sea wall towards the centre of these photographs, taken around 1898 and on Saturday 3 August 2002. At the time of the 'past' photograph the building was known as the Undercliff Hotel; in 2002 the well-known Spyglass Inn contains a fascinating collection of maritime memorabilia, and it is a unique experience to dine here with views out to the English Channel. The Esplanade was constructed in the late 1840s, and it can be seen that the beach was well stocked with bathing machines in the 1898 view, but even with these precautions bathing by ladies and gentlemen was segregated to different ends of the beach. Canoes and small sailing craft can be seen in the 'past' photograph; only small inflatable boats can be seen in the 2002 view. The empty deckchairs and the small number of people can be explained by the fact that I took the photograph among the first rumbles of thunder and tentative spots of rain from an approaching storm. *Isle of Wight Record Office/CH*

WHITWELL is a pleasant village situated between Ventnor and Niton. These photographs show the High Street around 1900 and on Saturday 24 August 2002, and the scene is readily recognisable in both views. The Methodist Chapel can be seen in the centre background. This was built in 1884 on land given by Lord Yarborough; while building was in progress services were held in a barn at nearby Whitwell Farm. It is recorded that people came from all over the Island for the opening service, but sadly this building has ceased to be used as a chapel in recent times, and in the summer of 2002 a planning application had been submitted to convert it into a private dwelling. The White Horse Inn, at one time an alehouse called Chiddles Cottage, can be seen on the left.

In 1887 Herr William Spindler, a German philanthropist who then lived at St Lawrence, donated half the cost of providing water standards throughout Whitwell, the water being piped from a source about half a mile west of the village. The balance of the cost of the installation was met by the villagers. One of these water standards remains near the chapel, and was also photographed on Saturday 24 August 2002. *Isle of Wight Record Office/CH*

ST CATHERINE'S ORATORY: In the early 14th century Walter de Godyton built a chapel high on St Catherine's Down. He also provided an endowment for a chantry priest whose duties included displaying lights to warn ships from coming too close to the dangerous coastline here. After the Dissolution the chapel was raided for the stone to be used as building material elsewhere, leaving only the lighthouse tower standing. In 1785 work commenced on building another lighthouse nearby, but this was not completed because it was realised that on this very high site the light would often be shrouded by mist or fog. Eventually a lighthouse was built in a lower situation close to the sea, but even here mist and fog caused problems – see opposite.

Now an attraction visited by many who enjoy walking, St Catherine's Oratory is seen undergoing conservation work in the 'past' photograph which probably dates from the 1950s. The 'present' view was taken during the afternoon of Monday 26 August 2002 and shows the tower looking for all the world like a medieval space rocket on its hill-top site. It also illustrates the changeable nature of the conditions at this exposed location; cloud and the beginnings of a cool mist coming in from the south-west can be seen on what had earlier been a beautiful summer day. *Isle of Wight Record Office/CH*

August 1948

ST CATHERINE'S LIGHTHOUSE is situated at Niton Undercliff at the southernmost point of the Isle of Wight. It is pictured during the 1930s and on Monday 26 August 2002. Construction of the lighthouse tower seen here started in 1838, following the loss of the sailing ship *Clarendon* on nearby rocks, and the lighthouse came into use in March 1840. This area is very prone to mist and fog, and it was found that the lighthouse had been built too high, frequently having its head in the clouds. In 1875 the light was lowered by removing segments from the middle and upper sections of the tower. This has resulted in the building having a slightly 'telescoped' appearance; the 'present' photograph has been taken from a slightly closer position to illustrate this more clearly.

During an air raid on 1 June 1943 the three keepers on duty at the lighthouse had taken shelter in the engine house. Tragically this was destroyed by bombing, resulting in the death of all three men; a plaque in their memory is displayed in the lighthouse.

Lighthouse keepers left St Catherine's Lighthouse for the last time on 30 July 1997 when it became fully automated, being controlled by the Trinity House Operations Centre at Harwich in Essex. The main light is visible for up to 30 nautical miles in clear weather, and is the third most powerful light under the control of Trinity House. *Isle of Wight Record Office/CH*

BRIGHTSTONE: These photographs compare the view looking east along the main road through Brightstone village in the early years of the 20th century and on Saturday 17 August 2002. The thatched building in the right foreground is readily recognisable in both photographs, and now serves as a newsagent, tobacconist and confectioner; it is pleasing to see this and the other shop (near the telephone kiosk in the centre of the 'present' view) still providing a service to local people in 2002.

As well as undergoing some rebuilding, it will be noticed that the New Inn in the centre of the 'past' photograph has now been renamed the Three Bishops. This is to commemorate three former Rectors of Brightstone who subsequently became Bishops – Thomas Ken (Bath and Wells, 1685-90), Samuel Wilberforce (Winchester, 1869-73) and George Moberley (Salisbury 1869-85). The church dates from 1190, and was originally quite small and without a tower. On the left of the 'past' photograph the church tower, added during the 14th century, can be seen; in 2002 the view of the church is obscured by the trees in the grounds of the hall in the left foreground. *Isle of Wight Record Office/CH*

NORTH STREET, BRIGHTSTONE: Dating from the 18th century and now owned by the National Trust, these cottages illustrate how buildings were constructed in the days before mechanical transport, when local materials had to be used. Built of chalk blocks and ironstone, both available close to the village, this row has a timeless external appearance that spans the centuries – a rural idyll indeed. The 'past' photograph was taken in 1972, and it is not surprising that hardly any changes are apparent when comparing this with the 'present' view taken on Saturday 17 August 2002. Part of the building closest to the camera is still the Post Office, but it will be noticed that two of the buildings further up the lane now also carry signs – for a National Trust shop and a Museum. Opened in 1994, the Museum is of particular interest, illustrating a number of aspects of life in Victorian Brightstone, including education, employment and home life. A visit is highly recommended! *Isle of Wight Record Office/CH*

The rural heartland

GODSHILL: This scene of All Saints Church and the thatched cottages at Godshill has to be one of the most visited and photographed places on the Isle of Wight. Legend has it that attempts were made to build a church on a site about a mile to the south of the present location, but the builders were frustrated by the nightly removal of their building materials to this hill-top site. After this had happened three times it was decided to build the church in this location, which became known as God's Hill. The church we see now was rebuilt during the 14th and 16th centuries. Visible in these photographs is the tower, which has required extensive repairs after being struck by lightning in 1778 and 1904.

The photographs compare the scene around 1930 and on Saturday 24 August 2002. Unsurprisingly very little has changed at this idyllic location – indeed, the two cars seen in the 'present' view look rather out of place. What is apparent is the number of visitors of various nationalities in the 2002 photograph, illustrating the continuing importance of the Island's tourism industry. *Isle of Wight Record Office/CH*

1948

HORRINGFORD STATION opened on 1 February 1875 with the line from Sandown to Shide (about a mile south of Newport). Completion to Newport, and connection with the line onwards to Cowes, was not achieved until 1 June 1879. For much of its route between Sandown and Blackwater the line followed the valley of the River Yar. On the Isle of Wight there are two water courses that rejoice in the name River Yar. As would be expected, one is in West Wight and meets the sea at Yarmouth, while the other rises near Merstone and flows via Horringford and Alverstone to reach the sea at Bembridge.

In the 'past' photograph, taken during the 1920s, a young lady stands on the river bridge, looking back towards the camera. Horringford station can be seen in the background, together with the level crossing gates. Despite being in a rather isolated location and relatively little used, it can be seen that the station is kept in excellent order; the white painted platform edge is especially noticeable.

The line from Sandown to Newport was closed on 6 February 1956, but the station building survives, now used as a private house – the roof line and chimneys can just be discerned among the trees in the 'present' photograph. The level crossing has long gone, and fencing now conceals the view of the building across the garden. On the afternoon of Saturday 31 August 2002 Marion Hawker stands in the same position as the lady in the 'past' photograph. *Isle of Wight Record Office/CH*

THE WHITE LION, ARRETON: Records of a settlement here go back to the 9th century. It is also known that a public house has occupied this site for over 400 years. In the 'past' photograph we see the White Lion around 1898, compared with the view taken from the same point on Saturday 31 August 2002. The premises were extensively rebuilt around 1900, transforming their appearance to that seen today. Notice, however, that the wall-mounted postbox has survived. Motor cars have replaced the bicycles and farm cart seen in the earlier view. However, there are those who maintain that spirits from the past continue to haunt the White Lion. Several people claim to have seen the ghost of a man wearing a hat and a long dark coat in a style from many years ago. Apparently when stared at or spoken to the apparition abruptly vanishes! This strange figure is said to have been seen both at the rear of the public house and in the lane nearby leading to the church. An interesting story, but given the location of the phenomena it could be speculated that the influence of a different type of spirit may have had some bearing on the observations! *Isle of Wight Record Office/CH*

ST GEORGE'S CHURCH, ARRETON: It is known that there was a place of worship on this site prior to the Norman Conquest, and in 1140 the manor and church at Arreton passed to the Abbey of Quarr. The church was then much smaller and had no tower. Enlargement was carried out by the monks, with the north aisle, prominent in both of these photographs, being added in 1160, although the pitched overall nave roof was not built until 1738. The west tower dates from 1299; there is a peal of six bells that vary in age from 1559 to 1951. In addition, the chancel was enlarged during the 13th century.

These photographs show the north side of the church and the west tower in 1955 and on Saturday 31 August 2002. As would be expected there have been few changes in the appearance of this historic building. Nonetheless during the years from the 1950s onwards electricity has been installed in the church, the roof has been re-tiled and the organ, installed in 1866, rebuilt. This is the only church dedicated to St George on the Isle of Wight, and during the last 20 or so years there has been a close link between this church and the Island branch of the Burma Star Association. A recent addition to the church (not visible in the 'present' photograph) is the Burma Star Memorial Window, which was unveiled by Countess Mountbatten of Burma on 12 May 1992. *Isle of Wight Record Office/CH*

WINKLE STREET, CALBOURNE, is another much-visited and photographed tourist attraction on the Island. Calbourne formed part of the Manor of Swainston, which passed to the Barrington family during the 16th century and remained with that family until 1832. The cottages seen in the photographs were built while the Barringtons were at Swainston, and were known as Barrington Row. This is still their proper title, although the better-known alternative name Winkle Street has been in common use since at least the 1920s.

These photographs were taken in 1920 and on Saturday 10 August 2002. A number of tourists can be seen in the modern view, but there have been few changes to the cottages. The parked cars, however, look distinctly out of place in this otherwise delightful rural scene. I suspect also that at least some of the cottages are now 'second homes' or holiday retreats, whereas in 1920 they would all have provided homes for local people. *Isle of Wight Record Office/CH*

SHALFLEET CHURCH is mentioned in the Domesday Book. The tower, prominent in both of these photographs, is the oldest part of the building and dates from the 11th century; the base walls of this massive structure are more than 5 feet thick. The nave dates from the 12th century, and during the late 13th century the south aisle, also visible in the photographs, was added.

A steeple was added to the tower in 1800 and can be seen in the 'past' photograph, which dates from around 1890. By the early years of the 20th century it was apparent that the extra weight of the steeple was too much for the tower, which had been weakened by opening an arch in its internal wall. The steeple was removed in 1912, but in 1914 part of the tower collapsed. Repairs were carried out in 1916, at which time the ivy seen in the 1890 view was stripped from the walls. Having carried no dedication for centuries, in September 1964 the church was dedicated by the Bishop of Portsmouth to St Michael the Archangel.

The 'present' photograph was taken on Saturday 10 August 2002. Now a Grade 1 listed building, extensive repairs are required to the south aisle. Inside the church the two-manual organ was built by a Mr Sims of Southampton and dates from 1886. *Isle of Wight Record Office/CH*

West Wight

FRESHWATER BAY is a semi-circular cove in the chalk cliffs on the south-west side of the Island. These photographs compare the view looking west around 1908 and on Saturday 7 September 2002. A number of Edwardian holidaymakers can be seen in the 'past' view; note also the bathing machines and the bathing tents dotted around on the rather rocky beach.

This little beach is still popular in 2002, and the provision of a promenade will be noted in the 'present' photograph. The building at promenade level is the Albion Hotel; it has been considerably extended since the 'past' photograph was taken, but it is still possible to discern the original buildings as the nucleus of the present structure. On higher ground behind the Albion, Freshwater Bay House is now used by HF as a base for its excellent holidays.

The Fort Redoubt on the headland was built in 1855-6 and remained in military use until it was sold in 1928. The former barracks was converted into a private residence in 1936, and subsequently a tea room has been built on the headland. *H. T. Glover collection/CH*

FARRINGFORD, a late-Georgian house near Freshwater, was home to Alfred, Lord Tennyson for nearly 40 years. Tennyson was appointed Poet Laureate in 1850 following the death of Wordsworth. Together with his wife and young son he rented Farringford in 1853; he subsequently bought the house in 1856. As the years went on the poet found that his fame carried with it the disadvantage of being pestered by tourists and autograph-hunters, especially during the summer months. In 1868 he had a second home built at Aldworth (near Haslemere) where he would live during the summer, returning to Farringford for the winter. It was on an October day in 1889 that Tennyson wrote his well known poem 'Crossing the Bar' after making the ferry crossing from Lymington to Yarmouth. When sung as a hymn to the lovely tune written for it by J. F. Bridge, this is my favourite piece of Tennyson's work.

After the death of Alfred, Lord Tennyson in 1892 Farringford remained in the Tennyson family and the 'past' view was taken during the early years of the 20th century. In 1947 the house was converted into a hotel, with additional cottages providing self-catering accommodation in the grounds. The building is readily recognisable in the 'present' photograph, taken on Saturday 17 August 2002; it is only the number of parked cars that gives a clue to Farringford's present-day function as a hotel. *H. T. Glover collection/CH*

TOTLAND BAY: This delightful little resort increased in popularity from the late 19th century onwards. The 'past' view is dated October 1924, while the 'present' photograph compares the scene on Saturday 10 August 2002. Totland Pier can be seen in the background of both photographs; opened in 1880, paddle-steamers and pleasure boats from such places as Bournemouth, Southampton and Portsmouth were soon calling here on their itineraries, and apart from the war years this continued until 1969. Breached during the Second World War, the pier was repaired and re-opened in 1951, and the building on the pier head seen in the 'present' photograph was added during the 1950s. Sadly the pier was forced to close after a safety inspection during the 1980s, but it has not been demolished and there are hopes that it may eventually be repaired and re-opened.

The gabled building in the right foreground can also be identified in both views. Now somewhat extended and modified, the building is used as a restaurant but was originally Totland's church until the present Christ Church was built in 1875; prior to becoming a restaurant the building was also used as a reading room.

The large building on the cliff-top in the 1924 view is the Totland Bay Hotel, which opened in 1880 and was extended in 1885. For many years it was a popular hotel, but fell victim to changing holiday habits in the post-war period, which eventually led to closure and demolition during the early 1970s. The provision of a concrete promenade will be noted in the 2002 photograph. *H. T. Glover collection/CH*

COLWELL BAY is a delightful bathing spot where the soft, sandy beach is popular with local people and visitors alike. These photographs compare the view around 1920 and on Saturday 10 August 2002. Prominent in the 'past' photograph is the hut from which Charles Conway hired out boats, canoes and bathing machines; similar facilities, together with swimming tuition, were also available from the Cole Brothers hut just visible in the left foreground. More enlightened attitudes mean that bathing machines have long since become obsolete, but it can be seen from the notice just visible in the foreground of the 'present' photograph that deckchairs and boats can still be hired at Colwell Bay in 2002. The provision of a concrete promenade will again be noted in the 'present' photograph.

Brambles Chine can be seen as the dip in the cliffs just to the right of the centre background; note the addition of Brambles Holiday Centre in the modern view. The large structure jutting out into the sea at the end of the cliffs is Fort Albert. As late as the 1950s this was still in military use, but it has now been converted into luxury flats.
H. T. Glover collection/CH

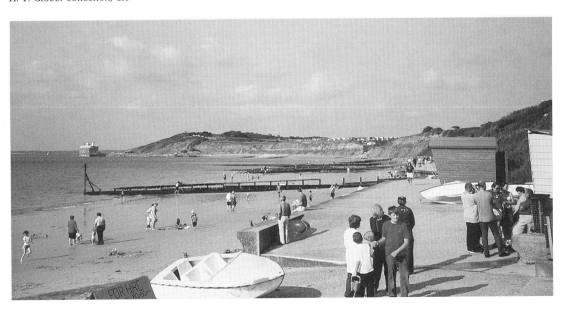

THE SQUARE, YARMOUTH: Many visitors to West Wight come by ferry from Lymington to Yarmouth. The name Yarmouth is thought to be derived from the Saxon word Ermud, meaning 'muddy estuary', and records of a settlement here go back to 1135. These photographs compare Yarmouth Square around 1902 and on Saturday 10 August 2002. A couple of horse-drawn carriages are the only vehicles to be seen in the 'past' view, and it was clearly safe for the dog to lie down in the road. When I took the 'present' photograph at 5.50pm I had to stand slightly further back than the photographer of yore so as not to risk ending up under a car!

The Bugle Hotel can be seen on the left of both views, while the tower of the Church of St James is prominent in the background. Built in the early 17th century, this beautiful church has some interesting stained glass windows, while the organ came second-hand from Boscombe Arcade in 1897. The clock, seen on the tower in both photographs, was installed in 1679.

Yarmouth Town Hall can be seen in the right foreground. The exact date of this building is uncertain, but it is thought to be pre-18th century. The exterior has changed little in the 100 years that separate the two photographs. The bunting across the road in the modern view nicely captures the happy atmosphere of the town on a summer evening. *H. T. Glover Collection/CH*

Transport of delight

DENNIS AND GUY DOUBLE-DECK BUSES: During the early years of the Company, Southern Vectis operated an all-single-deck fleet, many of the Island's roads not being considered suitable for double-deck buses. This led to the necessity of extensive duplication of journeys, especially during holiday periods, and in 1936 the Company took delivery of its first double-deck vehicles. These consisted of a batch of six Dennis Lance 2s, which carried 56-seat ECOC highbridge bodywork. Fitted with Gardner 5LW diesel engines from new, at first these buses were used mainly on the routes between Cowes and Newport or between East Cowes and Ryde. When fleet number 604 (ADL 504) was photographed at Ryde Esplanade towards the end of its service with the Company, it was operating on Service 20 between Ryde and Elmfield. ADL 504 was withdrawn in 1953, subsequently passing to a showman.

As would be expected for a Tilling Company, subsequent new purchases of double-deck buses were of the familiar Bristol/Eastern Coach Works configuration (see the following pages). However, a number of second-hand double-deck buses of other types also joined the fleet. One interesting example was BRD 754, one of the vehicles acquired with the Enterprise Bus Service of Newport in June 1951. Also fitted with a Gardner 5LW engine, this Guy Arab I carried a 55-seat Strachans lowbridge body built to the wartime Ministry of Supply utility specification. New to Reading Corporation in November 1942, this vehicle had come to Enterprise on the Isle of Wight in March 1950. Seen here on the service to Gurnard after acquisition by Southern Vectis, BRD 754 was withdrawn in November 1955. *Both Philip Davies collection*

A NICE PAIR OF BRISTOLS: The first Bristol double-deck bus bought by Southern Vectis was fleet number 700 (BDL 100). This Bristol GO5G carried 56-seat highbridge bodywork by Eastern Coach Works, and entered service in March 1937. It is seen here when new, displaying the pre-war Southern Vectis fleet name application. Withdrawn in October 1954, BDL 100 was sold to a dealer in Salford, and was noted with a showman in Scotland in 1968.

The post-war intake of Bristol K5Gs is exemplified by fleet number 713 (EDL 17), photographed at Ryde while operating Service 16 to Shanklin. EDL 17 carried the very attractive 55-seat lowbridge body by Eastern Coach Works then standard for that type of chassis, and entered service in March 1947. Notice the lower PV2 radiator and five-bay bodywork, compared with the high radiator and six-bay construction of the pre-war vehicle above. During the summer of 1963 this bus was loaned to Eastern National, and it was withdrawn in December of that year. *Both Philip Davies collection*

BRISTOL KSW5G BUSES: During 1952-3 Southern Vectis took delivery of 15 Bristol KSW5Gs with 55-seat lowbridge bodies by Eastern Coach Works. This attractive batch of vehicles is exemplified by fleet number 770 (JDL 720), new in June 1953 and seen here during the 1960s. JDL 720 was withdrawn by Southern Vectis in May 1970 and subsequently saw further service with Victory Tours of Sixpenny Handley, Dorset, before final withdrawal in July 1972.

By 1953 it was clear that there would be some contraction of the railways on the Island, which would add to the already heavy seasonal holiday traffic carried by the buses. With this in mind, most of this batch of KSW5Gs were fitted with full-length luggage racks along the nearside of the lower deck. Visually this balanced the protrusion of the upstairs gangway along the offside. The lower deck interior of fleet number 766 (JDL 40) was photographed by Philip Davies at Newport in June 1967. New in May 1953, this bus was withdrawn from service in May 1970. This type of semi-enclosed luggage rack on the lower deck of a lowbridge bus was very rare; the only other examples were on a small batch of buses for the Bristol Omnibus Company and on some lowbridge KSW double-deck coaches operated between London and Reading by Thames Valley.

Fond as I was of lowbridge buses, with their four-across upstairs seating, it has to be admitted that this type of bus suffered from a design fault that could potentially reduce the top-deck capacity by up to a quarter. There was a tendency for the bench seats to carry three very comfortable and well-spaced passengers, who would only grudgingly and reluctantly squeeze up to admit a fourth person if the bus was absolutely full! An experiment with a West Yorkshire vehicle in 1952 led to a new design of staggered upper deck seating, which overcame this problem. Eastern Coach Works

adopted the staggered seating layout as a standard in 1953, but by this time the writing was on the wall for the ECW lowbridge body with the advent of the Lodekka. The last five of the KSW5Gs delivered to Southern Vectis (JDL 719-723) had staggered upper-deck seats, but unfortunately I have been unable to trace an interior photograph of any of these vehicles. However, through the kindness of Mr Mike Penn of the Haynes Motor Museum, Sparkford, Somerset, I was able to photograph the upper deck of an identical Southern National vehicle (LTA 995) on Saturday 25 May 2002. *R. H. G. Simpson (Philip Davies collection)/Philip Davies/CH*

BRISTOL LODEKKA BUSES: One of the most significant advances in the development of the British double-deck bus was the advent of the Bristol Lodekka, which provided a bus only 13ft 4in high but with a centre gangway on both decks. Following a batch of pre-production vehicles in 1953, the Lodekka became generally available to the state-owned sector of the bus industry in 1954, and Southern Vectis immediately switched to the Lodekka for its ongoing deliveries of double-deck buses. Fleet number 543 (MDL 953) was an LD6G from the 1956 intake and is seen at Alum Bay when new, operating a Service 27 journey to Ryde. When delivered this bus had two-tier luggage racks over the offside rear wheel arch; by looking carefully this feature can just be discerned in the photograph, despite the reflection in the window. The rack was replaced by the more usual longitudinal seat for three passengers in 1960. MDL 953 was converted to open top in June 1973 and withdrawn in September 1978; a photograph of sister bus MDL 952 in open-top form can be seen on page 81.

At the end of the 1950s the Lodekka concept was further developed, with subsequent buses having virtually flat lower saloon floors and air rather than vacuum brakes. Known as the F series, the revised range of buses came into production in 1960. The most popular models with operators soon proved to be the 60-seat rear-entrance FS and the 70-seat front-entrance FLF. The FS was very similar to the LD it replaced, and thus a very attractive bus. However, I personally did not like the FLF, which seemed an awkward design compared with the traditional rear-platform double-deck bus. Southern Vectis, like most THC Group companies, took both FS and FLF examples. Fleet number 606 (BDL 582B) was one of the Company's first batch of FLFs; it was new in October 1964 and withdrawn in September 1982.

Both Philip Davies collection

BRISTOL VR BUSES: One-man operation using double-deck buses became legal in 1966. During that year Bristol and Eastern Coach Works had built two prototype double-deck buses with their engines mounted longitudinally behind the rear axle on the offside of the bus; the entrance was therefore ahead of the front axle, making the bus suitable for driver-only operation. However, in order to qualify for the new bus grants then available from the Government, production models, which came on stream in 1968, had the engine mounted transversely across the rear of the vehicle and the model was given the designation VRT, but has always been known to busmen as VR. Southern Vectis received its first VRs in May 1969. Fleet number 628 (SDL 638J) was one of the Company's 1971 intake and illustrates the flat windscreen fitted to Series 1 and early Series 2 VRs. In March 1987 this bus was repainted in the old Tilling-style Southern Vectis livery, and it is seen on 5 August that year at Ryde Bus Station, operating Service 1A to Cowes.

Later Series 2 and Series 3 VRs had an attractive curved wind-screen arrangement, as exemplified by fleet number 650 (MDL 650R), a Series 3 example new in August 1976. In 1979 this vehicle was repainted in the pre-1932 red and blue livery to commemorate the 50th anniversary of the Company. Seen here thus adorned, MDL 650R was repainted in National Bus Company green in March 1982 and withdrawn from service in October 1989. *David Smith (Philip Davies collection)/Southern Vectis collection*

GOING TOPLESS: As a prime holiday destination with much beautiful scenery, the Isle of Wight is an ideal location for the operation of open-top bus services during the summer months. Southern Vectis introduced its first open-top vehicles for the 1956 summer season, and for many years the open-top fleet consisted of a mixture of elderly second-hand vehicles with some of the Company's own older vehicles that had been converted for open-top operation. Examples of both can be seen in two photographs taken at Shanklin Bus Station in August 1961. DDL 50, seen in the top photograph, was new to Southern Vectis in 1940. This Bristol K5G with 56-seat highbridge bodywork by Eastern Coach Works was converted to open-top form by Southern Vectis in August 1959. Withdrawn from service in 1969, it was then used by the Company for tree-lopping. CAP 234, seen in the centre photograph, was acquired second-hand from the Brighton, Hove & District Omnibus Company in February 1960. This K5G also carried an Eastern Coach Works 56-seat highbridge body when new in October 1940, and was rebuilt as an open top by Brighton, Hove & District in 1954; at that time it had been fitted with the lower post-war-type radiator – compare with DDL 50 above. Notice also the sliding cab door, another 'Brighton' feature. I hope that the gentleman who has just reached the top of the stairs didn't lose his hat on the way to Ventnor! CAP 234 was withdrawn in 1967.

GL 6612, seen in the third photograph, is also a Bristol K5G. New to Bristol Tramways in May 1939, this bus carried a Brislington Body Works 56-seat body that had been converted to open-top form by Bristol in 1952. The different arrangement of the front destination box in particular will be noted. Acquired by Southern Vectis in November 1961, this bus entered service for the 1962 season, but served for only three summers with its new owner, being withdrawn in September 1964. *All Philip Davies collection*

MORE TOPLESS FROLICS: GLJ 969 was the youngest of a quartet of open-top buses that passed from Hants & Dorset to Southern Vectis in November 1964. When this Bristol K5G entered service with Hants & Dorset in October 1947 it carried a 55-seat lowbridge body by Eastern Coach Works, then in November 1957 it was given a 'new' open-top body. This had been constructed in the Hants & Dorset body shop in Southampton in 1953, and incorporated parts from a 1938 Brush body and possibly also from a wartime utility Strachans body. From 1953 until 1957 the resulting open-top body had been carried by Hants & Dorset fleet number 1019 (BTR 309). The photograph shows GLJ 969 in Bridge Road, Yarmouth, with a top deck full of happy passengers making for Alum Bay. Notice the full front (a quilt over the bonnet did its best to reduce the engine noise for the driver) and the standee windows. Withdrawn by Southern Vectis in 1973, this bus was later exported to the United States of America.

In high summer the 42 route includes the dramatic climb from Alum Bay to Needles Battery, and Bristol LD6G MDL 952 is seen climbing purposefully while the passengers enjoy the scenery on 22 August 1989. New to Southern Vectis in April 1956, this Lodekka originally had a two-tier luggage rack over the offside rear wheel arch in the lower saloon; this was replaced by the standard-type longitudinal seat in May 1960. Converted to open-top form in March 1973, this bus is seen in the predominantly blue 'Viewfinder' livery that it was given in May 1985.

In 1979 Southern Vectis acquired some modern one-man-operable open-top buses when six conventional Bristol VRs (UDL 671S-676S) were swapped for six convertible Hants & Dorset VRs of similar age (UFX 855S-860S). One of these ex-Hants & Dorset buses was photographed at work in Ryde Bus Station on Saturday 22 June 2002. Although still in Southern Vectis livery, UFX 858S is operating a circular open top service for Westbrook Travel. *R. H. G. Simpson (Philip Davies collection)/Philip Davies/CH*

THE OLD GIRL: No look at the open-top buses on the Isle of Wight would be complete without this well-known and well-loved vehicle. CDL 899 entered service with Southern Vectis in July 1939, and was the only double-deck bus bought new by the Company that year. A Bristol K5G, she carried a standard Eastern Coach Works highbridge body when delivered, but in 1959 was converted to open-top form by Southern Vectis. She has continued in use every summer thereafter, although limited to special occasions and private hires in recent years. Nonetheless she remains licensed and fit for use, and even carries the 'We Accept Euro Notes' vinyl in her top-deck front nearside window like her much younger closed-top double-deck sisters in the Southern Vectis fleet. And for the 2003 summer season there were plans for this venerable old lady to operate regularly on Service 41 (The Downs Tour), a circular service from Ryde including Wooton (for the Isle of Wight Steam Railway) and Robin Hill.

These photographs were taken during the Isle of Wight Bus Museum Running Day on Sunday 20 October 2002. Now restored to the livery she would

have carried when new, the exterior photograph shows how CDL 899 has retained her original high radiator; many early Bristol Ks were given the lower post-war type on rebuilding. Notice also the Autovac tank on the bulkhead. The only modern addition is the 'orange segment' flashing direction indicators, fitted in March 1971, while a tachograph (now required for private hire work) was fitted in 1982.

The lower-deck interior is similarly unchanged; notice the high window line in the front bulkhead to accommodate the high bonnet, and the half-drop side windows.

A view of the top deck is also shown; by their design it would appear that the seats currently fitted here date from the 1970s.

Known affectionately to staff as 'The Old Girl', CDL 899 has the distinction of being the oldest bus still in service with its original owner anywhere in the United Kingdom – and most probably anywhere in the world. *All CH*

DENNIS AND BRISTOL SINGLE-DECK BUSES: Southern Vectis purchased a number of Dennis Lancet single-deck buses during the 1930s. Illustrating the type we see fleet number 509 (DL 9009) at Ryde, ready to operate a Service 8A journey to Binstead. New in June 1934, DL 9009 carried a 36-seat ECOC body, which incorporated a sunshine roof and a roof-mounted luggage rack – standard features of Southern Vectis single-deck buses purchased between 1934 and 1938. Withdrawn in November 1950, DL 9009 passed to a showman in Hampshire and was eventually scrapped in January 1964.

Southern Vectis subsequently standardised on the Bristol chassis for new single-deck buses, a number of L5G saloons being taken into stock. From 1 June 1950 the maximum permitted length for a single-deck bus was increased to 30 feet, and Southern Vectis was quick to take advantage of these new dimensions; fleet number 834 (GDL 718) was new in November 1950 and was one of a batch of three Bristol LL5G saloons with 39-seat rear-entrance Eastern Coach Works bodies. Seen here laying over at Ryde after arrival on a Service 8 journey, GDL 718 was withdrawn in February 1963 and subsequently worked for a contractor before being scrapped in 1966. *Both Philip Davies collection*

BRISTOL RE BUSES: In 1962 a change in the Construction and Use Regulations permitted the use of buses 36 feet long in the United Kingdom. Around this time it was also evident that replacements would soon be needed for the large numbers of Bristol Ks put into service by the Tilling Group just after the Second World War. Bristol and

Eastern Coach Works saw the potential of the larger dimensions to introduce a single-deck bus that could carry almost as many passengers as a K, but which could be operated by the driver only – double-deck one-man operation was still illegal in the early 1960s. Production of the new model was under way by the mid-1960s, and a slightly shorter variant was also available, intended as a replacement for the MW, which was discontinued. Many older passengers had found single-deck buses with underfloor engines difficult to board because of the number and height of the steps that were needed. In this new design the engine was positioned at the rear of the bus rather than in the centre, thus allowing fewer and lower steps together with a gently ramped floor.

Early RE buses had a rounded body profile that was in many ways descended from the MW. An example is fleet number 810 (HDL 25E), which was new in February 1967. Seen here inside Shanklin Garage in June of that year, HDL 25E was one of the smaller RESL6G models, and seated 43 passengers. Withdrawn in September 1982, it was later used by Brymor Associates of Buckingham as a hospitality vehicle.

The more angular lines of the Series Two RE can be seen in the second photograph, of fleet number 866 (TDL 566K) operating Service 44 to Shanklin Esplanade in the mid-1970s. This bus was in service with Southern Vectis from January 1972 until March 1988. In the whole of the United Kingdom only two Bristol REs were converted to open-top form; one was used on the sea front at Scarborough in North Yorkshire, and the other was Southern Vectis fleet number 864 (TDL 564K). New in 1971, this bus was rebuilt as an open top in 1986 for use on Service 44. It was given the title 'Shanklin's Pony' with a special livery, which it still retains, as seen in this photograph taken at the Isle of Wight Bus Museum Running Day on Sunday 20 October 2002. *Philip Davies/Photobus/CH*

BEDFORD COACHES: After the Second World War most members of the Tilling Group standardised on the Bristol chassis for their new coaches. Although Southern Vectis did introduce some Bristol/ECW coaches, a number of Bedford vehicles were also brought into the coach fleet. The Bedford OB was a classic coach design of the immediate post-war period, and Southern Vectis took 16 of these vehicles into stock between 1947 and 1950. This batch of coaches is exemplified by fleet number 221 (GDL 796), new in June 1950 and seen here operating a 'Round the Island' tour during its early days with the Company. The Duple body had seats for 29 passengers. In 1958 its Bedford 3.5-litre petrol engine was replaced by a Perkins P6 diesel unit, and the vehicle was converted for use as a one-man-operated bus. Withdrawn by Southern Vectis in 1963, GDL 796 subsequently saw further service in Cyprus.

Four Bedford SBO coaches with 41-seat Duple bodies were taken into stock in March 1957. Fleet number 236 (ODL 49) is also seen on a 'Round the Island' tour. Notice how the fleet name has been placed in a small diamond (a representation of the shape of the Isle of Wight) within the moulding on the side. ODL 49 remained with Southern Vectis until 1967.

Southern Vectis was still buying new Bedford coaches in the 1960s. Fleet number 255 (ADL 108B) is one of five Bedford SB coaches with 41-seat Duple bodywork placed in service in June 1964. The stylish design of this vehicle allows the fleet name to be shown on the side in a rather more conventional Tilling fashion, and when photographed this coach was once again operating the 'Round the Island' tour. Withdrawn in September 1977, ADL 108B passed via a dealer to J. Smart Limited of Edinburgh, with whom it was in service until 1989. *H. T. Glover collection/R. H. G. Simpson (Philip Davies collection) (2)*

INHERITED COACHES: In May 1955 Southern Vectis took over the coach business of Bernard Groves of Cowes, providing it with excursion licences from that town. Four coaches were included in the take-over; three Bedford OBs dating from 1947-49, and this Bedford SB, seen unloading passengers while in service with Southern Vectis.

HDL 570 had been new to Groves in July 1951, and after passing to Southern Vectis in May 1955 was numbered 230 in the latter's fleet. The impressively bulky-looking body was built by Duple, and had seats for 33 passengers. Withdrawn by Southern Vectis in 1960, HDL 570 later worked for the Millbrook Steamboat & Trading Company and for Rule's Coaches of Boxford.

Southern Vectis acquired Nash's Luxury Coaches of Ventnor in 1956. This was a very old-established concern, dating back to 1887 when horse-drawn vehicles were operated from Ventnor Station. As well as premises in the town (see page 56), five coaches were added to the Southern Vectis fleet with the take-over of the Nash business, two of which are illustrated here in Southern Vectis livery. FDL 216 was a Dennis Lancet III with Duple 35-seat bodywork new in January 1948. As fleet number 101 it worked for Southern Vectis until 1959, and after withdrawal was exported for further use as a works bus on the Canary Islands.

Also acquired from Nash was GDL 32, a Crossley SD42/7 new in May 1949 with Whitson 33-seat bodywork. As fleet number 102, GDL 32 was in service with Southern Vectis until 1959. *The late R. F. Mack/R. H. G. Simpson(2), all Phillip Davies collection*

BRISTOL LS6G COACHES: The first underfloor-engined coaches to enter the Southern Vectis fleet were five Bristol LS6Gs with 39-seat Eastern Coach Works bodies. Two vehicles from this batch, new in July 1952, are illustrated here. Fleet number 304 (JDL 45) is seen in the Company's coach livery around 1960; this vehicle was converted by Strachans to a one-man-operated bus in June 1966 and withdrawn in September 1970.

Sister coach JDL 46 was similarly converted in June 1966, and was photographed in bus livery at Newport in June 1967. The front nearside quarter-light and pillar have been modified to enable a power-operated door to be fitted, while a bus-style destination box has been fitted to the front dome. Inside the vehicle the nearside front seat has been taken out to provide luggage space, reducing the seating capacity to 37. The rest of the coach seats remain, but with their head-rests removed. After withdrawal by Southern Vectis in May 1970, JDL 46 worked for Victory Tours of Sixpenny Handley, Dorset, before passing to a dealer in Barnsley in March 1973. *R. H. G. Simpson (Philip Davies collection)/Philip Davies*

BEHIND THE SCENES: All bus operators need a number of ancillary vehicles for use on various duties that are rarely thought about by passengers but are nonetheless essential to the smooth running of the undertaking. The top photograph shows a particularly interesting vehicle that was once part of the Southern Vectis ancillary fleet.

DL 9013 entered service with the Company in July 1934. It is a Dennis Ace, and when new carried Harrington bodywork with seats for 20 passengers. It was withdrawn as a bus in September 1954 and rebuilt as a lorry by the Company. The resulting vehicle is seen in use on route maintenance duties in June 1959 – the driver can just be seen working on the bus stop feature plate from steps beside the Bristol K in the background. DL 9013's origins as a bus are clearly visible, including the distinctive front end that caused buses of this type to be (affectionately) known as 'flying pigs'. Despite its immaculate appearance in the photograph, DL 9013 was taken out of service six months later and sold.

The lower photograph shows GXX 785, the heavy recovery vehicle operated by Southern Vectis from 1964 until 1986. Acquired second-hand through a dealer, GXX 785 is an AEC Matador dating from the mid-1940s. Preserved after withdrawal, this vehicle is shown on display at the Isle of Wight Bus Museum Running Day on Sunday 20 October 2002. *Philip Davies/CH*

LONDON, CHATHAM & DOVER RAILWAY CARRIAGES: Turning now to rail travel, the Isle of Wight at one time had an extensive railway network. This was always of particular interest in that the rolling-stock consisted of elderly carriages acquired second-hand from the mainland. This still applies on the surviving section of railway between Ryde and Shanklin – see page 92. Although steam operation by British Railways on the Island ceased at the end of 1966, we are fortunate that a section of line between Smallbrook Junction and Wooton, closed by BR on 21 February 1966, has been re-opened as the Isle of Wight Steam Railway. Using some of the original carriages, beautifully restored to their appearance in Southern Railway ownership, a trip on this line recreates the atmosphere of a train journey on the Island in days gone by.

Two of the most remarkable survivors are the carriages shown here, which were built by the London, Chatham & Dover Railway to a most unusual design that featured inward facing bench seats along the carriage sides. Originally built for use in schools' trains, by the early 1920s they were in use on the Isle of Sheppey Light Railway. After modification by the Southern Railway at Lancing Works, they were sent to the Isle of Wight in 1924. Carriage 6369, seen in the top photograph, is the older of the pair, having been built in 1887 as a 3rd Class saloon. The 1st Class compartment seen nearest the camera was created in 1924 when the carriage was adapted for use on the Island.

The lower two photographs show carriage 4112, which entered service in March 1898. On the Isle of Wight these carriages were normally employed on the branch from Newport to Ventnor West until withdrawn by the Southern Railway in 1938. The interior view of 4112 shows part of the unusual seating layout as well as the connecting door to the brake section. Sold locally after withdrawal, remarkably the grounded bodies survived to be restored by the Isle of Wight Steam Railway, where these photographs of the carriages at work were taken on Saturday 22 June 2002. *All CH*

LONDON, BRIGHTON & SOUTH COAST RAILWAY CARRIAGES: Coach 2343 was a four-wheeled carriage built by the London, Brighton & South Coast Railway in 1896. Originally used on services to the Crystal Palace in South London, it was renovated by the Southern Railway at Lancing Works in 1925 and shipped to the Isle of Wight, where it was mainly used on services between Newport and Freshwater. It spent a relatively short time in service with the Southern Railway on the Island, being withdrawn in 1931 and sold. Again the grounded body survived, and has been mounted on a new underframe and returned to service, lovingly restored by the Isle of Wight Steam Railway. These photographs show 2343 at Wooton on Saturday 22 June 2002; notice in particular the severe straight-backed seat and the basic internal door handle in the interior view. Note that even the non-smoking labels and the Guard's uniform are in authentic Southern Railway style.

Some more modern former LB&SCR carriages were transferred to the Isle of Wight during the 1930s. Carriage 2416 was built at Lancing Works in June 1916, being one of 24 former LB&SCR carriages shipped to the Island by the Southern Railway in May 1936. For many years used on trains between Ryde and Cowes, 2416 was later used between Ryde and Shanklin and remained in service until the demise of steam working on the Isle of Wight at the end of December 1966. It was one of the first carriages to be acquired for preservation by the Isle of Wight Steam Railway, and of course now works on part of its old regular haunt. Notice the original LB&SCR 'Smoking' signs etched into some of the compartment windows; the triangular 'No smoking' stickers are a 1950s British Railways design. The different types of door ventilators fitted to the coach are typical of how many carriages appeared in service on the Island in SR and BR days. 2416 was also photographed at Wooton on Saturday 22 June 2002. *All CH*

LONDON & SOUTH WESTERN RAILWAY LOCOMOTIVES: The elderly carriages used on the Isle of Wight railway system were complemented by equally venerable motive power. In the years following the 1923 Grouping the Southern Railway transferred a fleet of Adams 'O2' tank engines to the Island. Originally built by the London & South Western Railway for suburban and branch-line work, they were named after local towns and villages following their transfer to the Island, where they were to be the mainstay of the locomotive fleet for more than 40 years. Although some withdrawals had taken place as early as 1955, 14 of these Victorian locomotives were still in use at the beginning of 1966. Four were withdrawn during that year, but the final cull came on 31 December when the remaining passenger service between Ryde and Shanklin was suspended prior to electrification. All of the remaining 'O2s' were withdrawn and taken to Newport for scrapping, except for Nos 24 *Calbourne* and 31 *Chale*, which were retained for use on engineers trains. *Calbourne* survives in preservation and now works on the Isle of Wight Steam Railway, but *Chale* was cut up at Ryde in September 1967. To me these are two of the saddest photographs in the book. They were taken at Newport in May 1967, and show the 'O2' locomotives and other veteran rolling-stock lined up awaiting the breaker's torch. In the top photograph we see (left to right) Nos 20 *Shanklin*, 35 *Freshwater*, 38 *Ashley*, 17 *Seaview*, 33 *Bembridge*, 14 *Fishbourne* (the oldest locomotive in regular service on the entire British Rail network when withdrawn) and 22 *Brading*. The lower photograph nicely illustrates the extended bunker, a feature of these locomotives. Here the line-up is parked on the remains of the former Freshwater branch, closed in 1952. The old Newport engine shed can be seen in the background. *Both Brian Jackson Collection*

TUBE TRAINS ON THE ISLAND: The severely restricted loading gauge on the Island posed a problem when modernisation of the remaining line between Ryde and Shanklin was considered by British Rail. In 1966 some old London Underground carriages dating from 1923-34 were available after withdrawal from service on the Northern City Line, and their smaller size made them ideal for the Island; following refurbishment and conversion to the Southern Region third rail system, they commenced work between Ryde and Shanklin on 20 March 1967, the line having been closed since 1 January for electrification work. Already between 33 and 44 years old when they reached the Island, it was originally planned that these carriages would run for another ten years, so by the late 1980s, with some of the stock now over 60 years old, replacement was becoming urgent. The last of the 1938 stock was finally withdrawn from London Underground service in 1988, and British Rail bought a number of driving motor cars, which were converted to third rail operation, thoroughly refurbished and formed into two-car units for operation on the Island. Modifications have included the installation of fluorescent lighting and the fitting of a compressor to the D (Shanklin) end car of each unit. The first of the 1938-stock trains entered service on the Island in 1989 and all of the older stock was withdrawn by early 1991. Now 64 years old themselves, the 1938 trains continue to give good service, as these photographs taken at Ryde Pier Head during the afternoon of Saturday 22 June 2002 show. The London Underground ancestry of the stock is still obvious – especially from the interior, which also demonstrates that the trains are accessible for wheelchair users. The line was privatised in October 1996 and is now part of the Stagecoach organisation, branded as the Island Line. *Both CH*

THE LYMINGTON-YARMOUTH CROSSING: In 1884 the London & South Western Railway extended its Lymington branch from its 1858 terminus at Lymington Town to Lymington Pier, and also acquired the ferry route thence to Yarmouth. For many years operated by paddle-steamers with passenger accommodation only, by the 1930s increasing numbers of cars were also being conveyed by the rather inconvenient expedient of tow barges. In 1938 the Southern Railway introduced the first purpose-built car ferry on the route. This was the *Lymington*, built by Denny's of Dumbarton and able to carry 16 cars. In March 1948 she was joined by a superb (and unique) diesel-electric paddle vessel, the *Farringford*, also built by Denny's and with a capacity for 32 cars. The photograph shows *Farringford* arriving at Lymington Pier in the late 1950s; note the large number of passengers from the train, complete with luggage, who will catch the ferry for its return crossing to Yarmouth. A third vessel, the *Freshwater*, came into service on the route from September 1959, and *Lymington*, *Farringford* and *Freshwater* provided the service until 1973-4. Three new ships, *Cenred*, *Cenwulf* and *Caedmon*, identical to each other in design, were built by Robb Caledon of Dundee. *Lymington* was withdrawn after *Cenwulf* arrived in October 1973, while *Farringford* was transferred to the Hull-New Holland service early in 1974 and remained there until the Humber Bridge opened in 1981. *Freshwater* continued for a time as a relief vessel for this route and the Portsmouth-Fishbourne crossing.

The Lymington-Yarmouth route is a very pleasant way to reach the Island with a special atmosphere of its own. Something of this is captured in my photograph of *Caedmon* as she heads towards the mouth of the Lymington River on her way to Yarmouth as daylight fades during the evening of Saturday 28 September 2002. *R. K. Blencowe collection/CH*

RED FUNNEL: A popular route to the Isle of Wight is the crossing from Southampton to Cowes. Currently there are two routes operating from Southampton; a high-speed passenger-only service to West Cowes, and a conventional car and passenger ferry service to East Cowes. Both routes are operated by Red Funnel, which was properly called the Southampton, Isle of Wight & South of England Royal Mail Steam Packet Company Limited when the Company was formed by the merger of two existing shipping operators in 1861. Purpose-built car ferries were brought into service between Southampton and Cowes after the Second World War, with the first double-ended ferry, the *Netley Castle*, being introduced in 1972. For many years the ferry service ran from Southampton to West Cowes and East Cowes, but since the early 1990s the car ferries have run from Southampton to East Cowes, with Fountain Pier at West Cowes (see page 24) being served only by the high-speed passenger ferries.

Currently the car ferry service is operated by three modern vessels, *Red Falcon*, *Red Osprey* and *Red Eagle*. The top picture, taken from The Parade at West Cowes, shows *Red Osprey* on Saturday 20 July 2002. Launched in April 1994, she was built by Ferguson Shipbuilders at Port Glasgow and can carry 140 cars and 895 passengers.

The high-speed passenger service was introduced in the early 1970s, and until 1991 was operated by Italian-built hydrofoils. The newest of these, *Shearwater 6*, is seen in the centre photograph berthed at Southampton Town Quay on Tuesday 23 April 2002. *Shearwater 6* dates from 1982 and can carry 67 passengers with a speed of 32 knots.

In 2002 the Southampton to West Cowes service is normally in the hands of *Red Jet 1*, *Red Jet 2* and *Red Jet 3*. Built by FBM Marine at Cowes, *Red Jet 1* and *Red Jet 2* entered service in 1991, able to accommodate 138 passengers and travel at 35 knots. In July 1998 they were joined by *Red Jet 3*, which has a capacity for 190 passengers. The third photograph shows *Red Jet 2* departing Southampton for Cowes in the late afternoon of Tuesday 23 April 2002. *All CH*

TICKET TO RYDE: The shortest and quickest crossing to the Isle of Wight is via Ryde. Records of a steamship service between Portsmouth and Ryde go back to the 1820s. The railway Pier at Ryde was opened in 1880, and in that year the London & South Western Railway and the London, Brighton & South Coast Railway jointly acquired the ferry service between the two ports. Lots of people will remember with affection the paddle-steamers that operated this route for many years. A particular favourite was *PS Ryde*, which entered service in the summer of 1937. Requisitioned for mine-sweeping duties during the Second World War, she returned to the Portsmouth-Ryde route in July 1945. In the top photograph she is seen moored at Portsmouth on 9 October 1955. At that time the service was being worked by three paddle-steamers dating from the 1930s, together with three post-war motor vessels. The end of the paddle-steamer era came in September 1969 when *PS Ryde* was taken out of service; sold after withdrawal, at the time of writing she sadly lies derelict.

By the early 1980s the motor vessels operating the service were all more than 30 years old, and replacement was becoming urgent. In 1986 two high-speed catamarans, built by International Catamarans of Hobart, Tasmania, took over the service. Named *Our Lady Patricia* and *Our Lady Pamela*, these craft are scheduled to make the crossing in 18 minutes. They were supplemented by two additional catamarans, *Fastcat Shanklin* and *Fastcat Ryde* in 2000; these craft were built in Singapore in 1996 and had been used in the Philippines. The centre photograph shows *Our Lady Pamela* approaching Ryde with the 1320 crossing from Portsmouth on Saturday 18 January 2003.

The fastest journey from the mainland to the Island is provided by the Hovertravel link between Southsea, Clarence Pier, and Ryde Esplanade. Hovertravel was founded in 1965, and its service between Southsea and Ryde has proved very popular. The third

photograph shows AP1-88 hovercraft *Freedom 90* at Ryde on Saturday 28 September 2002, with Ryde Pier extending out to sea in the background. Built at East Cowes in 1990, *Freedom 90* can carry 96 passengers at speeds of up to 50 knots. The scheduled time for the crossing is 10 minutes, but this is sometimes bettered in calm conditions. *L. G. Marshall (R. K. Blencowe collection)/CH*

Index of locations